Real Estate
Investment Fundamentals

Deborah Long, DREI, EdD

www.apiexchange.com
— 1031 Advice
www.1031ITEC.com

Dearborn™
Real Estate Education

This publication is designed to provide accurate and authoritative information in regard to the subject matter covered. It is sold with the understanding that the publisher is not engaged in rendering legal, accounting, or other professional service. If legal advice or other expert assistance is required, the services of a competent professional person should be sought.

President: Roy Lipner
Publisher: Evan Butterfield
Managing Editor, Print Products: Louise Benzer
Development Editor: Anne Huston
Managing Editor, Production: Daniel Frey
Typesetter: Sheila Rose
Creative Director: Lucy Jenkins

Published by Dearborn™ Real Estate Education,
a division of Dearborn Financial Publishing, Inc.®
30 South Wacker Drive
Chicago, IL 60606-7481
(312) 836-4400
http://www.dearbornRE.com

Printed in the United States of America.

06 10 9 8 7 6 5 4 3

Library of Congress Cataloging-in-Publication Data

Long, Deborah H.
    Real estate investment fundamentals / Deborah H. Long.
        p. cm.
    ISBN 0-7931-8952-7
    1. Real estate investment. I. Title.
    HD1382.5.L658 2004
    332.63'24--dc22   2004008498

contents

Chapter 4   Types of Real Estate Investments   28

Chapter 5   Yield Measurements   39

Chapter 6   Understanding the Financial Management Rate of Return   47

During the 1970s, three real estate researchers began a search for a practical model to use to determine the desirability of real estate investments. Until that time, real estate educators had relied on such measurement tools as capitalization and equity dividend rates and the internal rate of return (IRR)—models that had significant shortcomings. In 1983, M. Chapman Findlay III, Stephen D. Messner, and Rocky A. Tarantello published *Real Estate Portfolio Analysis* (D. C. Heath and Company, Lexington, Mass.), a textbook that first introduced a complex new measurement tool they called the *financial management rate of return* (FMRR).

Since the publication of their text, the FMRR has been refined, expanded, adapted, and updated to reflect current tax laws and investment concepts. It has also been widely adopted by real estate educators and is considered by many to be the most sophisticated investment decision-making tool available. Because it is also one of the more complex measures of return, it often is not taught in prelicensing or postlicensing classes to the individuals who could obtain the most benefit from its use: real estate licensees working with investors. This course is an effort not only to simplify the FMRR so that real estate professionals can easily use it in their practice but also to review and evaluate other useful measurement criteria.

More than ever, real estate professionals are relied on for their expertise *outside* real estate because of the expectation of the public that they are versed not only in real estate issues but in alternative investments as well. This book familiarizes real estate practitioners with some of those alternatives. A caveat: real estate professionals are *not* financial planners, tax preparers, or attorneys. They should be prepared to recommend professionals who have the required skills and experience to guide their clients to the right decision. However, real estate professionals should be able to discuss, evaluate, and analyze investment choices with their clients in an intelligent and articulate manner. This textbook will guide the way.

Deborah H. Long, DREI, EdD, is a veteran educator in the real estate industry. Her areas of training expertise are ethics, e-commerce and the Internet, investment analysis, and cultural diversity. A Chicago native, Deborah has bachelor's and master's degrees from the University of Illinois and an EdS degree with emphasis in adult education. She completed her doctorate in educational leadership in 1994. Her doctoral research was on the effect of ethics instruction on the moral reasoning of Florida real estate students.

Deborah has been a real estate licensee for more than 25 years and has owned her own brokerage firm. She is also a licensed instructor in North Carolina and ten other states. In addition to holding GRI and CRS designations, Deborah is a DREI (Distinguished Real Estate Instructor), one of approximately 110 such teachers in the United States. In 2001, she was named North Carolina's Real Estate "Educator of the Year." In addition to being the editor of the *Real Estate Educators Association (REEA) Journal,* Deborah is the award-winning author of many articles and educational programs as well as 11 books.

Deborah provides continuing education programs nationwide, including seminars and workshops for Citibank, American Express, AT&T, the National Association of State Boards of Accountancy, the National Council of Interior Design, various state Societies of Professional Surveyors, the American Society of Mechanical Engineers, the National Council of Examiners for Engineers and Surveyors, the American Council of Engineering Companies, and numerous state boards and associations of REALTORS®.

Deborah lives in Chapel Hill, North Carolina. Her Web site is *www.deborahlong.com.*

acknowledgments

Real Estate Investment Fundamentals would not have been possible without the constructive feedback from my real estate students in my investment courses. I also wish to thank colleagues who provided insight and suggestions to enhance the readability of this book:

- Ignacio Gonzalez, Real Estate Coordinator, Mendocino Community College, Ukiah, Calif.

- Rick Knowles, Capital Real Estate Training Center, Austin, Tex.

- Paula Long, On Point Consulting, San Antonio, Tex.

- Joyce Bea Sterling, DREI, Northern Kentucky Real Estate School, Florence, Ky.

Dearborn Publisher Evan Butterfield encouraged me to write this book, and my editor Anne Huston gave me gentle advice along the way. I could not have written this book without the instruction of my real estate teachers and mentors who continue to guide me.

Finally, I wish to acknowledge the influence of my mother, who came to this country in 1945 as a penniless immigrant. By immediately enrolling in English/ GED classes and, by 1950, buying her first home with her earnings from making draperies, she taught me the value of two things: a love of education and the importance of owning your own home. Thanks, Mom.

chapter one

Investment Terminology

learning objectives

After completing this chapter, you will be able to

- appropriately apply the investment terms *yield, liquidity, marketability, leverage, risk, taxation,* and *management;*

- identify the characteristics of different types of investments, such as savings accounts, IRAs, stocks and bonds, mutual funds, business ventures, commodities, and collectibles;

- calculate the impact of leveraging on an investment; and

- determine if the impact of leveraging is positive, negative, or neutral.

■ Key Terms

buying on margin	liquidity	Ponzi scheme
investment strategy	management	risk
leverage	marketability	taxation
		yield

■ Introduction

In the late 1990s and into the new millennium, it became abundantly clear to investors that the stock market was a risky place to invest one's savings. Amateur and professional stock market investors saw their significant gains in the market during the 1990s evaporate and begin to erode their initial investment. Many of those same investors have now turned to real estate in the hope of finding a safer, more stable and long-term avenue for appreciation of their invested dollars. While no one investment type is 100 percent safe, real estate, when well chosen and managed, has been a solid long-term investment for many individuals who are not comfortable with the roller-coaster ride of more volatile investments.

■ Investment Terminology

Before investing funds, most investors consider several issues: for example, they may be concerned about safety because they may need the funds for retirement; they may consider whether they have the time to watch over the investment because they have limited spare time; they may be relatively young and have a long time before they have to sell the investment and liquidate.

To evaluate *any* investment, investors must consider the unique characteristics of each type of investment and then compare those characteristics in order to make a wise choice. While there are numerous investment criteria, let's focus on the significant ones: yield, liquidity, leverage, marketability, risk, taxation, and management.

Yield

A yield measurement, such as the *capitalization rate* or *equity dividend rate,* will tell investors how well an investment is performing. Yield measures the *return on* the invested dollar plus the *return of* the invested dollar. Clearly, investors would like the highest possible return. However, it is common to see yield inversely related to safety. In other words, the higher the yield of the investment (such as that offered by multilevel marketers), typically the higher the risk of the investment. Conversely, the lower the yield (such as that offered by most bank certificates of deposit), the higher the safety. (See Figure 1.1.)

Investors are entitled to *both* a *return on* and a *return of* invested dollars. Greedy investors sometimes overlook the risk involved in the promises of con artists who advertise 20 percent, 30 percent, 100 percent, and more *returns on* investment in a short period of time. Often those investment opportunities never give a *return of* the investor's original principal. Known as *Ponzi schemes,* these illegal pyramid schemes dupe thousands of people every year. Con artists use the "rob-Peter-to-pay-Paul" principle and use money from new investors to pay off earlier investors until the whole scheme collapses.

Figure 1.1 | Investment Yield

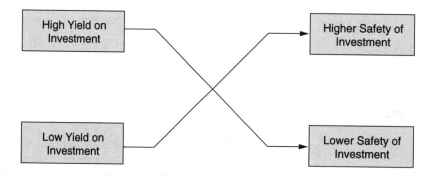

Charles Ponzi duped thousands of New England residents into investing in a postage stamp speculation scheme back in the 1920s. Ponzi thought he could take advantage of differences between U.S. and foreign currencies to buy and sell international mail coupons. Ponzi told investors that he could provide a 40 percent return in just 90 days, compared with 5 percent for bank savings accounts. Ponzi was deluged with funds from investors, taking in $1 million during one three-hour period—and this was 1921! Though a few early investors were paid off to make the scheme look legitimate, an investigation found that Ponzi had purchased only about $30 worth of the international mail coupons.

There are three yield measurements that will be discussed in this text: the *capitalization rate*, which is used by appraisers and cash investors; the *cash-on-cash* or *equity dividend rate*, which can be used for before-tax and after-tax cash flow analysis; and the *financial management rate of return* (FMRR), which is considered a very accurate measurement tool for long-term wealth building.

It is important to identify which yield measurement tool investors are using. When investors state that they want a 5 percent rate of return, it is important to know if they are referring to a 5 percent return on a cash investment, a 5 percent before-tax or after-tax return, or 5 percent based on one year's investment or an investment of several or many years. Knowing the yield tool is also important so that investors can compare one investment with another.

Liquidity

Liquidity is the ability to convert an asset into cash quickly with *little loss*. Real estate is an *illiquid* asset, while bank savings accounts are typically very liquid. For example, if investors purchased a residential fourplex property and a few months later determined that they wished to sell, it is extremely unlikely they would be able to extract all their invested capital. They would undoubtedly lose some of their principal. This loss would be likely to occur even months after their purchase. The loss could result from expensive marketing and closing costs incurred in the sale, and the situation could be worsened by a downturn in local real estate values.

Opening and subsequently closing savings accounts is much more likely to provide total liquidity. Banks routinely let their customers withdraw funds from their savings accounts; however, savings accounts have historically provided very low yields to their investors. So while a bank account may be liquid and relatively safe, only the most conservative investors would place a majority of their assets in such an investment. Bank certificates of deposits may not necessarily be completely liquid if banks charge a penalty for early withdrawal.

Leverage

Leverage is the ability to borrow/use assets to acquire investments. Several types of investments can be leveraged: for example, investors typically borrow the majority of their funds to purchase real estate. Investors in the stock market often use ownership of existing stock to buy more stock, an activity called *buying on margin*. Other investments do not lend themselves to leveraging. For example, to buy a $100 certificate of deposit (CD), an investor needs $100. To purchase antiques, investors need cash.

Using other people's money often has a desirable impact on yield, depending on the amount borrowed, the interest rate in borrowed funds, and the repayment terms of loan balance. For example, assume that investors paid all cash for a $200,000 investment that yields $28,000 each year after taxes. Their return would be 14 percent.

$$\frac{\$28,000}{\$200,000} = 14\%$$

Positive Leverage. It's unlikely, however, that investors would pay all cash for a real estate investment. Let's assume they borrow $160,000 of the $200,000 at 6 percent. Thus, they have to invest only $40,000 of their own funds or *equity*. Now what would their return be?

Positive Leverage

$200,000 × 14% =	$28,000	cash return
$160,000 × 6% =	− 9,600	annual interest payment
	$18,400	new return

$$\frac{\$18,400 \text{ new return}}{\$40,000 \text{ equity}} = 46\%$$

Because the investors' return went from a 14 percent return using cash to a whopping 46 percent return using borrowed funds, borrowing in this case is described as *positive leverage*. Positive leverage increases the property's rate of return.

Negative Leverage. Let's assume that interest rates are much higher—say, 15 percent (remember the 1980s?)—and again, our investors borrow $160,000 of the $200,000 for their real estate investment. Now what would their return be?

Negative Leverage

$200,000 × 14% =	$28,000	cash return
$160,000 × 15% =	− 24,000	annual interest payment
	$ 4,000	new return

$$\frac{\$4,000 \text{ new return}}{\$40,000 \text{ equity}} = 10\%$$

Because the investors return went from 14 percent using cash to only 10 percent using borrowed funds, borrowing in this case is described as *negative leverage*. Negative leverage decreases the property's rate of return. The resulting return may still be acceptable (a 10 percent return would be very acceptable to many investors), so investors may still go ahead and secure the loan. However, they may wish to consider decreasing the loan amount or finding better terms elsewhere.

Neutral Leverage.   It is possible for leveraging to have no impact on the property's rate of return. For example, let's say that our investors borrow $160,000 at 14 percent.

Neutral Leverage
$200,000 × 14% = $28,000   cash return
$160,000 × 14% =   − 22,400   annual interest payment
$ 5,600   new return
$$\frac{\$5,600 \text{ new return}}{\$40,000 \text{ equity}} = 14\%$$

Because the 14 percent rate of return achieved through borrowing funds is equal to the return achieved when paying cash, this event is termed *neutral leverage*. Neutral leverage does not affect the property's rate of return either positively or negatively. Investors may decide to borrow these funds because the lender is willing to take the risk, leaving investors with the cash in their pockets to commit to other investment projects.

Marketability

Marketability refers to how quickly assets can be sold at a price set by an active market. Many investments have a viable market where assets are traded. For example, the stock and commodities exchanges make it possible for traders to execute orders on a minute-by-minute basis. As another illustration, where once it was not easy for buyers and sellers of antiques and collectibles to find each other, now there are eBay and other Internet Web sites. Real estate can also be bought and sold relatively easily—particularly residential real estate. Residential brokers use a multiple-listing service (MLS) to provide an active, organized marketplace. Commercial brokers also use MLSs.

Investors often confuse the term *marketable* with the term *liquid*. While investments may be marketable—that is, they can be bought or sold easily—doing so *without a loss* can be challenging. Thus, real estate is marketable but not necessarily liquid. Remember that liquidity refers to immediate conversion to cash *without loss of capital*.

Risk

Risk refers to the uncertainty associated with expected investment performance. Virtually no investments are totally risk-free. Even keeping money under the mattress has some risk because a home can always be burglarized. Investors willing to take more risk and enjoy less safety may see higher returns on their investments. Investors who want more safety usually see lower yields.

Investment in real estate involves numerous risks: vacancy problems, natural disasters, local and national economic problems, and unexpected repairs are just a few possible risks. Other investment vehicles are similarly risky: investors in the stock market know that investing in some dot.coms in the 1990s put their capital in the dot.compost pile!

Taxation

Federal and state taxes can have a significant influence on investment performance. Some investments provide income that is tax-exempt (such as some bonds); some investments defer taxes on income (such as IRAs); others shelter a great deal of income from taxes (such as real estate income); some offer methods of avoiding taxes on the sale of the investment (again, real estate). Tax laws vary from state to state regarding investment income and the sale of investment assets; federal tax laws also change periodically. While tax laws have changed the *degree of tax shelter* that real estate investments provide, there still remains an opportunity to shelter real estate investment income from taxes. Residential real estate is slightly favored by federal tax laws over commercial real estate investment. Further, profits made from the sale of a long-held real estate investment are now taxed at a relatively low (15 percent or 5 percent) capital gains rate. Clearly, the impact of taxation depends on the taxpayer's individual circumstances and the type of investment. While taxes should never be the most important consideration in a taxpayer's decision to invest in any investment, the potentially profound impact is a critical issue for any investor.

Management

While some investors are particularly sophisticated in managing their investments, most investors need and/or want professional assistance. Management deals with the amount of effort required to find the investment and to manage it. Real estate can be a relatively intense asset from the standpoint of management. Investors must make decisions regarding the type of investment (residential, industrial, commercial), timing of sale, whether to make improvements, leveraging considerations, maintenance, and tenant relationships. Investors who do not have the time or knowledge to make these types of decisions can, of course, always hire professional property managers, keeping in mind that the decision to hire professional management will have an impact on yields because management can be expensive.

Some investments do not require as much time: savings accounts and mutual funds are attractive alternatives for people who do not want to think about their investments. These investments are managed by others, who presumably have the time and the knowledge to make sound decisions. Of course, savings accounts offer low yields, and mutual funds have some risk. Among the lessons learned from the stock market in the 1990s is that even professional funds managers can make serious investment mistakes.

■ A Final Note

Purchasing any type of investment can have a profound impact on the investor's future. Investors should consider having an *investment strategy,* that is, a plan that will help them meet their financial goals, whether their objectives are to save for a child's college expenses or for retirement. In many cases, investors need professional assistance in developing their strategy for maximizing their future wealth. Professionals who help develop those strategies are often tax preparers, such as certified public accountants (CPAs), tax attorneys, and financial planners, as well as others, such as real estate professionals and stockbrokers, who may render specialized assistance. (For more information on professionals who assist with financial planning, see the Web links following the summary.)

■ Summary

Each type of investment—real estate, savings accounts, business opportunities, stocks and bonds—has unique characteristics. For investors to make an appropriate choice for their portfolios, they should compare those characteristics in order to make a wise choice. The significant investment characteristics are yield, liquidity, leverage, marketability, risk, taxation, and management.

Of these investment characteristics, the ability to borrow other people's money, or leverage, is often considered critical because leveraging can have an impact on the other factors, such as yield and risk. When the cost of borrowing money is relatively low, positive leveraging may occur. When the cost of borrowing money is relatively high, negative leveraging may occur. Neutral leveraging occurs when borrowing money does not have a significant impact on the investment's return when compared with the return if the investor paid cash.

In the next chapter, we will look at these investment criteria and apply them to a variety of investment opportunities available to investors.

■ Web Links

American Institute of Certified Public Accountants. *www.aicpa.org*

Financial Planning Association. *www.fpanet.org/*

National Association of REALTORS®. *www.realtor.org*

National Association of Securities Dealers. *www.nasd.org*

National Society of Accountants. *www.nsacct.org/*

■ Chapter 1 Review Questions

1. *Capitalization rates* or *equity dividend rates* are examples of
   a. marketability.
   b. yield measurements.
   c. liquidity.
   d. risk tools.

2. Illegal pyramid schemes using the "rob-Peter-to-pay-Paul" principle are referred to as
   a. Peter-Paul schemes.
   b. Cairo schemes.
   c. Ponzi schemes.
   d. All of the above

3. The use of other people's money is known as
   a. marketing.
   b. liquidity.
   c. investing.
   d. leveraging.

4. Which of the following criteria should be used to evaluate an investment?
   a. Yield
   b. Liquidity
   c. Leverage
   d. All of the above

5. The ability to convert assets into cash quickly *with little loss* is known as
   a. marketability.
   b. taxation.
   c. liquidity.
   d. risk.

6. Which of the following is a liquid asset?
   a. Real estate
   b. Stocks
   c. Bonds
   d. Savings account

7. Positive leverage occurs when
   a. the interest rate on a loan is lower than the projected rate of return if the investors paid cash.
   b. the interest rate on a loan is higher than the projected rate of return if the investors paid cash.
   c. the interest rate on a loan is equal to the projected rate of return if the investors paid cash.
   d. None of the above

8. Investors who are willing to take more risk may see
   a. lower yields.
   b. lower returns.
   c. higher yields.
   d. higher vacancy rates.

9. Which of the following investments is completely risk-free?
   a. Real estate
   b. Stocks
   c. Savings accounts
   d. None of the above

10. With regard to the management of real estate investments, which of the following is FALSE?
    a. Real estate can be a relatively intense management asset.
    b. Management decisions involve the type of investment, timing of sale, whether to improve the property, leveraging considerations, maintenance, and tenant relationships.
    c. Investors who do not have the time or knowledge to manage their own properties can hire professional property managers.
    d. Hiring property managers has no impact on a real estate investment's yield.

chapter two

Investment Alternatives

learning objectives

After completing this chapter, you will be able to

- discuss and evaluate the investment characteristics of savings accounts and IRAs;

- distinguish between Roth IRA, traditional IRA, Coverdell Educational Savings Account, SEP-IRA, and SIMPLE;

- discuss and evaluate the investment characteristics of stocks and bonds and mutual funds; and

- discuss and evaluate the investment characteristics of business ventures, commodities, and collectibles.

■ Key Terms

cash equivalents	futures contract	Roth IRA
commodity	futures trading	SEP-IRA
Coverdell Educational Savings Account	individual retirement account (IRA)	SIMPLE
credit risk	maturity date	traditional IRA

■ Introduction

Investors today face bewildering choices for investing their disposable income. Their choices range from relatively safe but low-yielding investments to highly risky but potentially high-yielding alternatives. Real estate professionals are similarly challenged to keep up with the array of choices so that they can speak intelligently about the merits (or demerits) of these investment choices in comparison with real estate.

Table 2.1 | Evaluating Investment Possibilities

Type of Investment	Yield	Liquidity	Marketability	Leverage	Risk	Taxation	Management
Savings (including CDs, money markets, T-bills)							
IRAs							
Stocks							
Bonds							
Equity Mutual Funds							
Business Ventures							
Commodities							
Collectibles							
Real Estate							

■ Investment Possibilities

Investors today have a great number of choices in which to place their surplus funds: savings accounts, money market accounts, CDs, a variety of IRAs, mutual funds, and so on. It's likely that real estate agents will find themselves having to defend real estate as an appropriate investment choice to potential investors, even though most of them will have had a good experience owning real estate before—as homeowners. Real estate professionals should be prepared to discuss the advantages and disadvantages of real estate as an investment and to contrast it with other investment vehicles. However, real estate professionals should also advise their clients to discuss the details and impact of purchasing any investment with the appropriate financial adviser.

Evaluating Investments

Before we begin a formal discussion of the characteristics of various investment possibilities, use Table 2.1 to evaluate the following investment vehicles based on the characteristics defined in Chapter 1. Use the modifiers *good* or *positive, bad* or *negative,* or *ok* or *neutral* in your assessment of the yield, liquidity, marketability, leveraging opportunities, risk and taxation factors, and management issues. Evaluate these investments based on your past experience or knowledge.

Table 2.2 represents the evaluations of these investment vehicles by investment professionals. Compare your answers in Table 2.1 with this table and with the responses of other students, keeping in mind that these responses are subjective.

While there are bound to be disagreements in the evaluation of these different investments, take note: Did your chart affirm that real estate compares favorably with other investments? It is likely that you evaluated real estate as *good* in all but two categories: liquidity and management. No other investment opportunity fares as well when we review all of the characteristics. In this chapter, we review the characteristics of the alternative investment choices in the chart above.

Table 2.2 | Responses to Evaluating Investment Possibilities

Type of Investment	Yield	Liquidity	Marketability	Leverage	Risk	Taxation	Management
Savings (including CDs, money markets, T-bills)	Poor	Good	Good	Poor	Good	Poor	Good
IRAs	Good	Poor	Good	Ok	Poor	Good	Ok
Stocks	Good	Poor	Good	Good	Poor	Poor	Poor
Bonds	Good	Poor	Good	Poor	Ok	Ok	Good
Equity Mutual Funds	Good	Poor	Good	Good	Poor	Poor	Poor
Business Ventures	Good	Poor	Poor	Poor	Poor	Ok	Poor
Commodities	Good	Poor	Good	Poor	Poor	Ok	Poor
Collectibles	Good	Poor	Good	Poor	Poor	Poor	Good
Real Estate	Good	Poor	Good	Good	Good	Good	Poor

■ Savings Accounts

Investors who wish to invest in cash can put money into bank accounts and money market mutual funds or can buy what are known as *cash equivalents:* U.S. Treasury bills, certificates of deposit (CDs), and similar investments. Some investors do not think of bank accounts as investments because they currently pay such a low rate of interest, but technically, any time money is used to make more money, it is investing.

Investment in money markets includes short-term, highly liquid, relatively low-risk debt instruments sold by governments, financial institutions, and corporations to investors with temporary excess funds to invest. This market is dominated by financial institutions, particularly banks, and governments. The maturities of money market instruments range from one day to one year and are often less than 90 days.

Another investment in cash is the Treasury bill (T-bill) as a benchmark asset. Although in some pure sense, there is no such thing as a risk-free financial asset, on a practical basis, Treasury bills are risk-free because they are sold by the U.S. government. There is no practical risk of default by the U.S. government. Treasury bill rates are lower than the rates available on other money market securities, approximately one-third of a percentage point, because of their risk-free nature.

Issued in exchange for a deposit of funds by most American banks, the CD is a marketable deposit liability of the issuer, who usually stands ready to sell new CDs on demand. The deposit is maintained in the bank until maturity, at which time the holder receives the deposit plus interest. Maturities typically range from 14 days (the minimum maturity permitted) to one year or longer.

In summary, money market instruments are characterized as short-term, highly marketable investments, with an extremely low probability of default.

■ Individual Retirement Accounts

An individual retirement account (IRA) is a retirement savings plan that allows individuals to save for retirement (or for college) on a tax-deferred basis. The portion of the invested amount that is tax deductible varies according to an individual's access to pension coverage, income tax filing status, and adjusted gross income.

There are different types of IRAs: Roth IRAs, traditional IRAs, education IRAs, SEPs, and SIMPLEs.

Roth and Traditional IRAs

The most significant advantage of Roth IRAs is that while investors contribute to them on an after-tax basis, they have the opportunity to withdraw their earnings on a tax-free basis, assuming certain conditions are met. The ability to make a full contribution to a Roth IRA is limited, based on an employee's income.

Investors realize the greatest tax advantage from traditional IRAs (or non-Roth IRAs) when they can make contributions on a deductible (pre-tax) basis. However, many public sector employees are not eligible to make fully deductible (pre-tax) contributions to a traditional IRA. If investors or their spouses do not actively participate in an employer-sponsored retirement plan, they may make fully deductible contributions to a traditional IRA regardless of their income. All taxpayers under age 70½ with earned income are eligible to make nondeductible contributions to a traditional IRA.

Education IRAs

Education IRAs are now called *Coverdell Education Savings Accounts.* A Coverdell Educational Savings Account is a trust or custodial account that is created exclusively for the purpose of paying the qualified higher education expenses of the designated beneficiary of the account.

SEPs (Simplified Employee Pensions)

A SEP is a written arrangement or plan allowing an employer, including self-employed individuals, to make contributions toward his or her own and employees' retirement plans without becoming involved in more complex arrangements. The contributions are made to a traditional IRA for each participant of the plan, hence the term *SEP-IRA.* Each participant under the SEP may establish his or her own IRA at the institution of his or her choice. As the underlying account is an IRA, any covered employee may have a self-directed IRA as his or her SEP-IRA. This is in addition to any other IRAs one has.

SIMPLE (Savings Incentive Match Plan for Employees of Small Employers)

A SIMPLE plan is a tax-favored retirement plan that employers with 100 or fewer employees (including self-employed individuals) can set up for the benefit of their employees. Called SIMPLE IRA, for Savings Incentive Match Plan for Employees, employees can make salary deferral contributions, and employers must make a contribution as well.

Most investors choose to invest conservatively in their IRAs because those funds will be needed for retirement or education. Those investors with a longer time-line, say, a 22-year-old, may choose more aggressive instruments (such as growth stocks) for an IRA than a 50-year-old (who may choose cash instruments or bonds). IRAs are not liquid because of penalties for withdrawals. However, IRAs can be easily managed (by banks, for example, or by other IRS-approved entities, such as mutual fund managers) and are favorably treated by the IRS. Their yield is entirely dependent on the types of investments in the IRA.

■ Stocks

An investor in stocks is a part owner of the corporation that issued the stock. In the past, stocks have offered one of the greatest long-term investment returns, largely because of the strength of the U.S. economy as reflected in the growth of U.S. corporations and the price appreciation of corporate stocks.

When a company prospers, investors who own its stock can make money in two ways: current income, if the company pays part of its earnings to shareholders as dividends, or capital appreciation, if the price of its shares increases. Because there is no limit on how much a company can earn or how high its stock price can go, there is no limit on how much return a stock investment can provide. Similarly, there is no limit on how long investors can own a stock and continue to benefit from its increasing value through either dividend income or price appreciation.

Stocks, also known as *equity investments* because they give investors ownership, can pose risk as well as the opportunity for profit. Their prices fluctuate in response to what is happening in the company that issued the stock, in the industry of which the company is a part, and in the economy as a whole.

So while investing in stocks gives the investor a marketable asset, stock is not usually a liquid asset. Witness the excess of day trading in the 1990s and the losses that some investors experienced in less than a few hours. However, the appeal of stock investment continues to be the potential for high yield. Investors must either be sophisticated and vigilant enough to know when to buy and sell or hire a stockbroker or adviser for help.

■ Bonds

Bonds are financial obligations of corporations, governments, or government agencies. The issuer usually pays periodic interest to the bondholder and is obligated to repay the value of the bond at a specified time (known as the *maturity date*). Short-term bonds normally have maturities of less than one year. Intermediate-term bonds normally mature in from two to ten years. Long-term bonds normally run more than ten years.

Bonds are generally described as less risky investments than stocks, because investors usually hold bonds until maturity, at which time they get a stipulated return both on and of their investment. The risk investors take—in addition to the possibility that rising inflation will undercut the buying power of the interest income investors earn—is that the issuer may not be able to meet its obligation to pay the interest and repay the investment. This is known as *credit risk.* However,

Table 2.3 | Average Total Return of Stocks Versus Bonds

	Stocks		Bonds	
	Total, %	% per Year*	Total, %	% per Year*
The 1950s	486.5	19.4	10.5	1.0
The 1960s	112.1	7.8	18.1	1.7
The 1970s	76.8	5.9	83.1	6.2
The 1980s	398.1	17.4	240.2	13.0
The 1990s	432.3	18.2	132.4	8.8

*Compounded.
Source: Reproduced with permission of Value Line Publishing, Inc.

because bonds are rated by independent rating companies, investors can buy highly rated bonds that pose virtually no danger of default. Because bonds constantly fluctuate in value, if investors need to liquidate a bond investment during its term, they might have to sell for less than they paid.

Bonds are generally considered a smart way to diversify an investment portfolio, because in most years they perform differently from stocks, and in some periods when stocks are depressed, bonds can provide a positive return.

Table 2.3 illustrates the average total return of stocks over five decades, as shown by the S&P 500 Stock Index and corporate bonds, based on the Salomon Brothers Bond Index. With the exception of the 1970s, stocks outperformed bonds.

■ Equity Mutual Funds

Equity mutual funds are regulated investment companies that do not have their own commercial operations. This means that they do not manufacture or sell products or services to customers. Their purpose is to purchase and manage portfolios of stocks in various companies for the benefit of the funds' shareholders. There are now literally thousands of equity mutual funds, and their numbers continue to increase.

Mutual fund investors typically want to put their capital in the stock market but do not know enough to choose their own stocks. Essentially, mutual fund investors are individuals who hire a professional investment manager. Mutual funds are offered by investment companies, banks, trust companies, credit unions, insurance companies, and professional organizations. The main advantages of mutual funds are professional management and investment diversification. Mutual funds are generally regarded as long-term investment and typically have specific objectives. Some may concentrate on speculative growth investments, others on preservation of capital and a steady income.

Mutual fund portfolios may include common stocks, preferred shares, bonds, Treasury bills, precious metals, and real estate in any combination. Day-to-day investment decisions are made by the fund manager, who decides the asset mix within the objectives of the fund. Professional management, diversification, and long-term gains are the benefits of mutual funds.

■ Business Ventures

So you want to start your own restaurant? Been dreaming about operating your own discount office supply store? Want to go head-to-head with eBay and start your own online auction house? Starting a new business demands much more than a good idea. Starting a new business is a high-risk venture, particularly if the owners and/or operators of the business are inexperienced, disorganized, or lacking in necessary business skills.

First, a new business needs seed capital, which means that owners/operators must also convince a wide range of people that the idea is a good one and that profits can be generated in the future.

There are a number of other issues to consider in starting a new business: funding (bank loans, venture capital, investment from family and/or friends, and/or independent wealthy individuals looking for investment opportunities) is perhaps the most significant challenge to new business operators. Sometimes local or national grants are available. Similarly, grants and tax breaks are also available for specific locations, such as enterprise parks.

Many businesses take a year or longer to make a profit, requiring that owner-investors have other sources of funds for living expenses. It's important to have a business plan to project income and expenses as well as to get the attention of banks, venture capitalists, and other investors. Initial expenses will be very high relative to income: office space, furniture and other equipment, marketing and advertising, and personnel are just some of the expenses that start-up business owners must face.

Some investors in business prefer to buy an existing business or invest in a franchised operation. There are risks here as well. Why is the existing business for sale? It's important to have the financial savvy to read the current owner's accounts and determine the relative health of the business.

Purchasing a franchise can mitigate some of the problems new business owners face because franchisors typically offer training to new owners and act as a resource when new problems surface. But franchisees pay a significant part of their revenues to the franchisor for this benefit.

Needless to say, running a business can also be time- and labor-intensive. A successful business, however, can bring satisfaction, opportunities for growth and expansion, and a tangible asset that can be sold in the future.

■ Commodities

What is a *commodity*? Some examples are products you commonly see and use on a daily basis:

- Corn in breakfast cereal
- Lumber in furniture
- Gold in jewelry
- Cotton in clothing
- Steel in cars

- Crude oil for the gasoline that runs a car
- Wheat in sandwich bread
- Beef and potatoes in the dinner meal
- Currency used to buy all these things

These commodities and many more are traded among thousands of investors, every day, all over the world. They are all trying to make a profit by buying a commodity at a low price and selling at a higher price. They do this by investing in *futures trading,* which involves speculating that the price of a commodity will go up or down in the future. Futures trading is mainly speculative paper investing, that is, it is rare for the investors to actually hold the physical commodity. Instead, they hold a piece of paper known as a *futures contract.*

A futures contract investment has an expiration date. Investors don't have to hold the contract until it expires. They can cancel it anytime. Many short-term traders hold their contracts for only a few hours—or even minutes! Expiration dates vary among commodities, so investors must choose which contract fits their market objective.

How Futures Contracts Work

Investor Roberta assumes that gold will rise in price until mid-August. Today is June 30. The gold contracts available are February, April, June, August, October, and December. Because it is the end of June and the June contract has already expired, investor Roberta would choose the August contract. If she thought the price of gold would rise until September, she would choose the October contract because a September contract doesn't exist.

Futures are highly leveraged investments. An investor has to put up only a small fraction of the value of the contract (usually around 10 percent) as *margin.* In other words, investors can trade a much larger amount of the commodity than if they bought it outright, so if they have predicted the market movement correctly, their profits will be multiplied (tenfold in this case). The margin required in holding a futures contract is not a down payment but a form of deposit. If the market goes against the investors' positions, they may lose some, all, or possibly more than the margin they have put up. (You may remember the Dan Ackroyd / Eddie Murphy movie *Trading Places* [1983] where both the heroes and the villains of the movie lose a great deal of money trading orange juice and silver commodities.) Thus, investing in commodities is considered potentially high-yielding but at equal or greater risk than other investments. Management of commodities is also an issue because traders must keep a vigilant eye on the market at all times.

■ Collectibles

Investing in collectibles such as antiques, art, coins, Barbie dolls, and Beanie Babies also requires expertise. The joy of investing in such items is that the investor has physical ownership of an item that may be not only beautiful to look at (or entertaining to own) but may also appreciate in value over time. In recent years, thanks to the success of online Internet auction houses such as eBay, collectibles have also become more marketable because buyers and sellers of such items have a much easier time connecting with one another. The disadvantage of collectibles investing is that in some cases, the collectible can be reproduced, thus adding to the supply of the item and diminishing its value.

Generally, it is those genuine one-of-a-kind antiques or no-longer-manufactured collectibles that tend to retain value and even appreciate. If investors have little or no expertise in investing in such items, they have to hire art brokers and specialists. Further, there may be some management problems with investing in collectibles (such as storing valuable art), and there is no favorable tax treatment given on gains made on the sale of collectibles. Nevertheless, investing in collectibles remains a favorite interest and even a hobby of many investors who enjoy the items they collect, regardless of yield or other pecuniary benefits.

■ Real Estate

Since real estate investment is the focus of this text, we will examine its various characteristics in depth in Chapter 3.

■ Summary

In addition to the investment possibilities described above, there are many other investment vehicles, such as insurance annuities, real estate investment trusts, gold, and precious metals. Investors should always be advised to consider those investment opportunities that best match their investment strategy and to seek the counsel of financial experts.

Investors who seek safe, albeit low-yielding, investment should consider savings accounts and other cash equivalents in their portfolios. Those investors who need tax-deferred instruments should consider individual retirement accounts (IRAs) but be aware of eligibility factors. Stocks provide growth and income possibilities but may have more risk than bonds. Investors who wish to invest in the stock and bond markets but do not have time or expertise may consider mutual fund investing. Business ventures, commodities, and collectibles may be appropriate investments for those who can handle risk and management issues. As will be discussed in the following chapter, real estate investment compares favorably to these investment alternatives in terms of yield, marketability, leveraging opportunities, risk, and taxation.

■ Chapter 2 Review Questions

1. Education IRAs are now called
   a. SEPs.
   b. SIMPLEs.
   c. Roth IRAs.
   d. Coverdell IRAs.

2. The steel in cars and the crude oil that they use are described as a
   a. commodity.
   b. business venture.
   c. collectible.
   d. government maturity.

3. All of the following are cash equivalents EXCEPT
   a. U.S. Treasury bills.
   b. money market mutual funds.
   c. equity mutual funds.
   d. certificates of deposit (CDs).

4. "A cash asset sold by the U.S. government at auction that is virtually risk free" is a description of
   a. stocks.
   b. bonds.
   c. Treasury bills.
   d. certificates of deposit.

5. Futures are considered
   a. low-risk investments.
   b. highly leveraged investments.
   c. a method of investing in collectibles.
   d. a method of buying Treasury bills.

6. The best kind of IRA for taxpayers who do not meet income eligibility standards is the
   a. Coverdell Education Savings Account.
   b. education IRA.
   c. Roth IRA.
   d. traditional IRA.

7. An option for investors who want to put their capital in the stock market but do not want to choose their own stocks would be
   a. money market securities.
   b. bonds.
   c. mutual funds.
   d. collectibles.

8. If investors have little or no expertise in investing in collectibles or antiques, they should
   a. not invest in such items.
   b. hire brokers and specialists.
   c. invest in bonds instead.
   d. invest in business ventures instead.

9. All of the following are true regarding mutual funds EXCEPT
   a. mutual funds investors are individuals who hire a professional investment manager.
   b. mutual funds are offered by investment companies, banks, trust companies, credit unions, insurance companies, and professional organizations.
   c. the main advantages of mutual funds are professional management and investment diversification.
   d. mutual funds are generally regarded as *short-term* investments and typically have *general* objectives.

10. The paper certificate indicating an ownership of commodities is called a
    a. franchise contract.
    b. futures contract.
    c. collectible.
    d. business venture.

Real Estate as an Investment

learning objectives

After completing this chapter, you will be able to

■ evaluate real estate investments in terms of permanence, scarcity, government influence, taxation, and marketability;

■ describe the advantages of real estate as an investment in terms of appreciation potential, leveraging opportunities, personal control and involvement, use of inside information and skill, and tax consequences; and

■ describe the disadvantages of real estate as an investment in terms of loss of value due to external and internal factors, unexpected expenses, loss of tax advantages, management problems, lack of liquidity, large capital requirement, and risk.

■ Key Terms

environmental risk	legislative risk	operating financial risk
interest rate	operating business risk	

■ Introduction

As discussed in Chapter 2, real estate as an investment compares favorably with other investment alternatives. However, real estate professionals should be able to discuss the potential disadvantages of real estate investments as well as its favorable characteristics.

■ Real Estate Investment Characteristics

Permanence

Real estate, unlike stocks, is a relatively permanent, fixed, and durable investment. Its permanence is the very reason financial institutions are willing to lend money on such investments. Unlike other types of movable collateral (cars and boats), real estate doesn't "go" anywhere, making it easy for lenders to seize this asset in the event of a foreclosure. Its permanence is also the reason why lenders are willing to provide funds for 10, 20, or 30 years and more.

Real estate's permanence is also why investors find it attractive. Income streams derived from tenants can be projected into the future with some degree of accuracy. Furthermore, the longer the income stream can be guaranteed, the more value the property has. Real estate's permanence, however, also means that it is subject to the whims and fortunes of the local market. If you invest in a single-family home in Houston, you can't pick the house and land up and move it to Florida if the Texas economy tanks. Thus, investing in any parcel of real estate necessitates careful analysis of the local market, including political and economic activities in the vicinity of the investment.

Real estate's permanence also suggests that investment in land and improvements is a long-term proposition. While some TV pitchmen suggest, "You can make a million dollars in real estate overnight!" in fact, real estate investments can take several years to break even, and significant income, positive cash flow, and profit may come only in ten years or more.

Scarcity

Unlike collectibles, which can be in limitless supply (such as Beanie Babies), real estate is a relatively scarce commodity. As American humorist Will Rogers once said, "Buy land! They ain't making any more of it." There will always be a demand for good real estate, thus causing well-chosen real estate investments to appreciate.

Supply and demand causes real estate values to go through cycles. For example, when a new subdivision is created, the neighborhood goes through rapid growth. As the homes sell, eventually the growth cycle slows and plateaus. Over a long period of time, as homes start to require maintenance and investment, there may be a period of decline. When prices drop, new owners move in and fix up the properties, causing a recovery during which values begin to increase again. While this cycle is dependent on many factors and is influenced by local issues, over long periods of time, real estate values tend to increase.

Government Influence

Many government activities can influence the short-term and long-term value of real estate. As an example, the federal government controls the supply of money and, thus, interest rates. Fortunately for homeowners and investors, interest rates have remained well below 10 percent since the 1990s, making it possible for more American households to own their own homes than ever before and for investors to experience positive cash flow earlier from the rental properties in their portfolio. However, real estate practitioners who were counseling clients in the 1980s remember all too well when interest rates were 15 percent and higher. (See Figure 3.1.) When rates go up, the cost of supporting higher mortgage payments causes investors to reach into their own pockets to support their investments' expenses. Further, when mortgage interest rates go up, values diminish because borrowers cannot qualify for loans. Sellers accept lower offers on their properties. The supply of real estate increases, further causing values to drop.

Figure 3.1 | Historical Mortgage Interest Rates

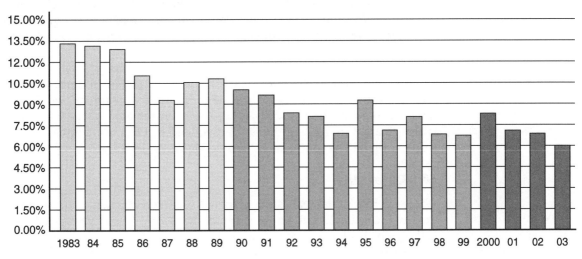

Source: Data obtained from *www.hsh.com/mtghst.html.* © 1983 – 2004 by HSH Associates

In the new millennium, average interest rates on 30-year fixed mortgages are the lowest they have been since the early 1990s. While this decrease brought joy to residential tenants who could now afford to buy their own homes, it distressed landlords because it became difficult to attract tenants. Rents decreased precipitously in many residential markets. Commercial builders also borrowed "cheap money" in record amounts, adding to an oversupply of office space, also causing rents to drop.

While controlling the money supply is one example of how government policy can affect real estate investment value, environmental controls and policies are another. Many federal and local programs limit growth, particularly in environmentally sensitive areas. Some communities have established moratoriums on growth altogether. Scarce supplies of water or fear that growth will cause contamination of water or air are other concerns related to real estate development. As an illustration, one landowner/developer in Chapel Hill, North Carolina, had to wait more than three years to begin a large residential subdivision until engineering and impact studies could demonstrate the development's influence on air, water, traffic, and school conditions. Such research reports and time delays cost investors a great deal of money and time. Local political attitudes toward zoning and growth also have a significant impact on land value.

Taxation

Real estate investment can be an attractive addition to an investment portfolio because of the potential for tax shelter. Tax shelter can be achieved by the investor's ability to

- avoid capital gain taxation on the profit of the investment when it is sold,

- avoid income taxes on the annual cash flow generated by the investment, and

- avoid income taxes on other earned income because of the investment's excess losses.

Virtually all of a rental property's operating expenses are tax-deductible. For example, property repairs, advertising expenses, taxes, and insurance are all write-offs. While taxpayers cannot deduct the principal paid on an income property's mortgage, they can deduct the interest, which is the lion's share of the mortgage payment.

Tax laws also allow real estate investors to depreciate the building. While depreciation allowances are not nearly as generous as they were under pre-1986 tax laws, depreciation deductions still allow taxpayers to save money. There are many rules and regulations regarding the tax consequences of real estate investment ownership, which will be completely discussed in Chapters 6 and 7.

Marketability

While the residential real estate market is relatively organized, its organization is mostly local. Residential agents typically belong to a multiple-listing service (MLS), which allows them to find sellers and buyers easily. Other real estate markets, such as industrial and commercial, are not as organized. Real estate professionals in these market sectors use social and professional networking opportunities as a method of brokering transactions.

It is difficult to organize real estate because the product itself cannot be standardized. Every parcel of real estate is unique. No two properties are identical. Unlike other markets where the product has a fixed price and/or a fixed unit (such as stocks and bonds), real estate varies in quality and quantity, and its price is subject to negotiation.

■ Advantages of Real Estate Investment

While investing in real estate can be risky and poses potential downsides to investors, the advantages of real estate investment are significant as well: appreciation potential, leveraging opportunities, personal control and involvement, opportunities to use inside information and skills, and beneficial tax consequences.

Appreciation Potential

In most areas, real estate investments, particularly single-family homes, increase in value. The increase depends on many factors, of course, such as those discussed earlier. Appreciation in value above the rate of inflation is good news because it represents an increase in real wealth.

The census provides information about housing appreciation. According to the 2000 census, the median value of houses more than doubled in the last 50 years, although the most significant growth occurred more than two decades ago.

In the 1950s, the median value of housing increased in value to $58,600, representing a 31 percent increase over the previous decade. That value increased to $65,300 in the 1960s, an 11 percent growth. Between 1970 and 1980, the median value of single-family, owner-occupied houses grew by 43 percent from $65,300 to $93,400. In the 1980s, housing experienced its lowest rate of appreciation of any decade since 1950—8.2 percent. The median price grew to $101,100. In the 1990s, the value grew 18 percent to $119,600, according to Lew Sichelman in "Most Explosive Appreciation Came during the 1970s," *Realtytimes.com* (July 30,

2003). (Individual regions and states have appreciation figures that vary from national averages.)

Leveraging Opportunities

In today's "easy money market," in which loanable funds are in strong supply and interest rates are low, financing real estate investments has never been easier. Even FHA loan programs permit qualified borrowers to buy investment property up to four units with little down payment if they occupy one of the units. VA programs permit qualified borrowers to purchase investment property with no money down under similar restrictions.

Where investors are nonoccupants, typical lending terms require that they invest 20 percent to 25 percent in the down payment. Fixed-rate mortgages for 30 years or longer are readily available, making it easier for rental income to cover mortgage payments. Leveraging opportunities and long-term loans make real estate investment profitable with minimum investment.

Personal Control and Involvement

Unlike other investments such as stocks, bonds, and collectibles, investors can exert some measure of control over the performance of their investments. Knowledgeable landlords can choose tenants wisely, make repairs and improvements in a timely manner, and maintain effective rent policies. When landlords do not have this expertise, they can choose good property management firms to guide them.

Use of Inside Information and Skills

Many investors put their occupational skills to good use in real estate investments. Handy individuals, carpenters, and electricians can add significant value to their properties by applying their building skills. Teachers and psychologists can use their gifts in dealing with people to choose good tenants. Attorneys and accountants have experience in effectively negotiating lease terms and/or handling income streams, respectively. Just being a primary residential property owner gives a beginning investor an edge because property owners know some of the maintenance issues in taking care of their own homes.

Real estate agents may use their knowledge of the market to enter into transactions on their own behalf as well. However, because of licensing laws and fiduciary obligations they may have to clients, agents *must* and/or *should* disclose their license status when they are acting as buyers or sellers in a transaction. If real estate licensees make these disclosures, there is nothing unlawful about their investing in real estate themselves. In fact, real estate professionals who own real estate investments can offer the benefit of their experience to their clients, thus making themselves more valuable to consumers. Many real estate professionals make good real estate investment counselors. Some will even choose to specialize in this field and will take advanced coursework and/or earn designations such as Counselor of Real Estate (CRE).

Beneficial Tax Consequences

As discussed earlier in this chapter, tax laws can have a positive impact on the investment performance of real estate. Most real estate investment properties can shelter not only the income they generate but other income earned by the owners. Furthermore, current tax laws allow investors to pay a relatively low capital gains tax on the sale of profit or to defer taxes by getting involved in a 1031 tax-deferred exchange. Chapters 6 and 7 discuss the impact of tax laws on real estate investors.

Disadvantages of Real Estate

Real estate has fewer disadvantages than other types of investments, but real estate professionals should not minimize these issues. Disadvantages include loss of value due to external factors, loss of value due to internal factors, unexpected expenses, loss of tax advantages, management problems, lack of liquidity, large capital requirement, and risk.

Loss of Value Due to External Factors

While property owners have some degree of control over the value of their investment by proper management, they rarely have control over local matters, much less regional or national economies. For example, a local zoning board may make ordinance changes, allowing nearby land and structures to cause a decline in value for other properties. As another illustration, local employment factors can change, causing potential tenants to leave the area, leaving values and rents depressed.

Loss of Value Due to Internal Factors

The movie *Pacific Heights* illustrates the problems associated with loss of value due to internal factors. In this film, a disturbed tenant moves into a San Francisco three-story apartment building, disrupting the lives of the owner-occupants and their tenants. Tenants may destroy or abuse property, refuse to pay the rent, and/ or refuse to vacate the property.

Owners and property managers who defer maintenance can cause the property to lose its appeal and value as well. Witness, for example, the significant increase in problems associated with mold, largely due to property owners ignoring moisture intrusion in their structures.

Unexpected Expenses

As the adage goes, "expect the unexpected" when it comes to real estate expenses. Sometimes tenants destroy property, causing an unexpected expense (and the wrath of the landlord). Sometimes weather events, such as hurricanes and tornadoes, contribute to unforeseen expenses. Many building components have a relatively short life and wear out quickly, such as appliances and carpeting. Longer-lived components, such as roofs, once fully depreciated, are very expensive to replace.

Loss of Tax Advantages

Tax laws can change on Congress's whim. Under recent administrations, real estate ownership and investment have been treated favorably. However, many real estate professionals remember the terrible 1980s, when capital gains taxes were much higher and depreciation allowances became less generous.

Because tax laws can change, investors should not buy real estate purely for its tax-sheltering qualities.

Management Problems

Real estate investors can spend a great deal of time managing their properties. Management involves such activities as collecting the rent, maintaining the property (mowing the lawn, clearing common areas of unsafe conditions, garbage removal), finding tenants, and negotiating leases. The time spent in management tasks can increase dramatically with poor tenant selection. Management problems can be somewhat reduced by hiring professional property managers, but even then, owners must check the property on a regular basis to make sure that property managers are doing their jobs.

Lack of Liquidity

In Chapter 1, *liquidity* was defined as the ability to quickly convert an asset into cash without any loss in value. Real estate is *not* a liquid asset. If real estate owners are forced to sell quickly, they may have to sell at a discount, particularly if the sale takes place within a short time of the purchase or during a bad market period.

Large Capital Requirement

Even though it is possible to purchase a real estate investment with little or no money down, investors are more likely to have to come up with enough cash for a down payment *and* closing costs, in addition to enough funds to pay for immediate repairs or improvements to the property and to cover any shortfall in income. These expenses can easily run to five or six figures.

Risk

Real estate investment is subject to substantial risk, as the projected income may not be produced and the original investment may not be returned. Real estate also requires more management than other investments. In addition, undertaking and closing a sale may require substantial time, thus affecting both marketability (the ability to sell an asset in a viable marketplace) and liquidity (the ability to sell an asset for the amount paid for the asset).

Other elements of risk are associated with the life cycle of real estate (its performance over the course of time) and the entry point of the investor (the point in the cycle at which the investment is made).

The risk that actual income may be lower than projected and expenses may be higher is known as *operating business risk.* This would be a significant risk for an office or apartment building but not for a land investment.

The risk that available financial resources such as loans and savings may be insufficient to fund operations is known as *operating financial risk.*

Interest rate risk is related to changes in interest rates. If the interest rates available in the market increase, the value of the investment would decrease because it would be more expensive to finance the investment. If the interest rates available in the market decrease, the value of the investment would increase because it would be less expensive to finance the investment.

Substantial costs may be required to conform to new environmental protections unknown at the time the investment was made. Wetlands protection, endangered species protection, and other environmental issues are some concerns that contribute to *environmental risk.*

Legislative risk is the possibility that legislative changes could require additional costs for future investments or could actually increase the value of investments that were made prior to the legislative changes. Examples include tax laws enacted by Congress or, at the local level, land use changes or zoning law amendments.

■ Summary

Real estate investors prefer minimizing risk, preserving their capital, and earning a profit. Real estate investments offer relative safety, good appreciation and leveraging opportunities, tax-shelter possibilities, and a high degree of personal control compared with other types of investments. While real estate is illiquid compared with other investments, investors who choose to place their money into a long-term real estate vehicle will often be rewarded.

■ Web Links

Counselors of Real Estate. *www.cre.org*

Federal Housing Administration. *www.hud.gov*

Department of Veterans Affairs. *www.va.gov*

■ Chapter 3 Review Questions

1. Real estate investments have all of the following advantages EXCEPT
   a. leveraging opportunities.
   b. liquidity.
   c. appreciation.
   d. personal control.

2. When the supply of real estate increases
   a. rents go up.
   b. demand goes down.
   c. values go down.
   d. values go up.

3. Depreciation deductions
   a. benefit the taxpayer.
   b. are less generous than they have been in the past.
   c. can change by an act of Congress.
   d. All of the above

4. "Loss of value due to internal factors" could refer to
   a. a rise in interest rates.
   b. a weather-related loss.
   c. bad tenants.
   d. local environmental policy.

5. The risk that actual income may be lower than projected and expenses may be higher is known as
   a. leveraging risk.
   b. operating business risk.
   c. investment risk.
   d. inflation risk.

6. It is difficult to standardize real estate as a product because
   a. many regions of the country do not have a multiple-listing service.
   b. real estate is sold in a regulated market.
   c. each parcel of real estate is unique.
   d. brokers are opposed to the standardization of the marketplace.

7. During periods of low interest rates, builders tend to
   a. stop building.
   b. add to the oversupply of buildings.
   c. add industrial buildings to the market.
   d. apply for unemployment insurance.

8. The typical cycle for neighborhoods is
   a. growth, plateau, decline, recovery.
   b. recovery, decline, plateau, growth.
   c. growth, plateau, recovery, decline.
   d. decline, plateau, growth, recovery.

9. All of the following are advantages of real estate investment EXCEPT
   a. detrimental tax consequences.
   b. personal control.
   c. leveraging opportunities.
   d. appreciation potential.

10. All of the following are disadvantages of real estate investment EXCEPT
    a. loss of value due to internal factors.
    b. illiquidity.
    c. personal control.
    d. risk.

Types of Real Estate Investments

learning objectives

After completing this chapter, you will be able to

- contrast the qualifying questions asked of a prospective homebuyer with those asked of an investor;

- describe the characteristics of different types of investment real estate;

- evaluate investors based on a variety of qualifying factors; and

- appropriately use the terms *initial investment, gross, percentage* and *net lease, generative function, suscipient function,* and *weight-gaining* and *weight-reducing operation.*

■ Key Terms

generative function	net lease	weight-gaining operation
gross leases	percentage leases	weight-reducing
initial investment	suscipient function	operation

■ Introduction

Qualifying an investor is a different process from qualifying a prospective home-buyer. Among the questions that a real estate professional must ask a homebuyer are "How much cash do you have for this purchase?" "How far is your commute to work?" "What amenities do you need in your home?" "Are there any particular features of a home you want or need?"

With the exception of the first question regarding cash requirements, none of these inquiries is particularly relevant for qualifying prospective investors. Not only must real estate professionals ask the right questions but they must also provide advice on the appropriate investment property. Real estate professionals should strive to make a good match between the investor's needs and what the investment property will provide.

Investment property considerations should include

- types of investment property;
- purchase price and terms;
- available financing;
- cash flows, positive or negative;
- tax implications;
- current and potential conditions of the property;
- management and maintenance issues;
- vacancies and collection problems;
- expected income and operating expenses; and
- short-term and long-term yield.

Types of Investment Property

There are many different types of investment properties available to investors. It is important for real estate practitioners to know the characteristics of these properties so that they can give appropriate advice to their clients and make a good match between the client and the property. Investors can choose among residential properties (single-family homes, multiunit apartment rentals, and condominiums), office buildings (lowrise and highrise buildings, office parks, and office condominiums), shopping centers (neighborhood, community, regional, and superregional shopping centers), industrial properties, and specialty investments (mobile-home parks, motels, golf courses, and nursing home or adult congregate living facilities).

Residential Properties

Single-Family Homes

Residential properties provide investment opportunities for both small and large investors. Single-family homes as rental properties are a good first real estate investment for novices who are familiar with the challenges of maintenance and mortgage payments. However, single-family homes can be difficult to manage. In good economic times, potential tenants buy their own homes. If the single-family rental property is vacant, landlords must dip into cash reserves to cover mortgage payments and maintenance.

Single-family homes are relatively easy to sell, however, compared with multifamily structures. They also tend to retain their value and appreciate, particularly if there are not too many rented single-family homes in the area. Remember: location, location, location. For a single-family tenant, good views, nice landscaping, neighborhood amenities, and availability of transportation for commuting to and from work are important aspects of renting.

Multifamily Apartments

Rental apartments are a popular form of residential investment property. Duplexes, triplexes, and larger apartment structures that vary in amenities, design, price, and profitability can be found in all major communities. One of the advantages of owning rental properties, say, a fourplex, is that if one unit is vacant for a period of time, the other three units are still bringing in income to cover mortgage payments and other expenses.

However, apartment building tenants multiply maintenance issues. In a four-unit apartment building, there may be four times more waste, repair, and collection problems. The greater the number of units, the more likely it is that a landlord will require the services of a professional manager. The good news is that the larger the apartment complex, the more likely professional property management is an affordable option.

Another potential disadvantage of owning apartment buildings is that they tend to sell more slowly than single-family homes.

Landlords use *gross* or *flat leases* with residential tenants, requiring them to pay a flat amount per month. Landlords typically pay taxes and insurance, while utilities and maintenance tend to be negotiable.

Condominiums

Condominiums offer many of the advantages of single-family homes. They also may provide an advantageous location plus amenities. The investment opportunities are similar to those for single-family home development. However, many condominium owners must abide by a condominium association's strict rules regarding tenant occupancy, including limits on how often owners may rent their units. Investors should check the homeowners' association's *protective covenants* regarding rental policies before buying condos with the intention of renting them.

Federal, State, and Local Laws

Residential landlords must be particularly alert to federal, state, and local fair housing laws, which are designed to eliminate discrimination in the sale or rental of housing because of race, color, religion, sex, national origin, handicap, or familial status. While there are limited exemptions for some landlords regarding discrimination under federal fair housing, by and large, landlords and their agents should offer dwelling units with no restrictions that may be interpreted as based on the seven protected classes mentioned above. Furthermore, local fair housing laws may be even stricter than federal or state laws and may have eliminated the exemptions.

The majority of states have residential landlord-tenant laws that prescribe appropriate rental terms and dwelling conditions. Communities may also have building codes that prescribe minimum living conditions. Rent control laws that are prevalent in many urban as well as suburban communities could be a major concern to prospective investors if they cannot raise rents to offset increased expenses.

Violations of any of these laws could result in significant fines and even jail time.

■ Office Buildings

The need for office space has steadily increased as the U.S. economic base has shifted from farming to industry to service businesses. Many commercial operations such as corporate headquarters and professional services are housed in offices. The central business districts attract many of these interrelated businesses, such as banks, accounting firms, and law offices. Lawyers and accountants who service outlying areas often prefer locations on main arteries. Medical offices are frequently located near hospitals. Corporate headquarters for industrial firms are following a trend of moving to the suburbs where taxes are lower and commuting time is shorter.

Office investment is available in a variety of sizes and types: small office buildings to large ones, office condominiums, and office parks. No matter the type of office building, finding tenants and keeping them happy is a critical priority for investors. Most businesspeople prefer signing long-term leases because they don't want to change business addresses often. To attract good long-term tenants, office landlords typically provide rental concessions such as tenant improvements (customizing office space) and full-service management (janitorial services). Good parking, street visibility, and a good mix of tenants are also important for office landlords, particularly in the case of smaller office buildings.

Larger office buildings may offer full-service secretarial or business centers, health clubs, and restaurants. These types of properties are found in central areas of cities, although some may be found in populated suburban areas. Typically, a highrise structure is designed around a major tenant that takes the majority of the office space.

The investment attraction of office buildings is based on the tax benefits and stability of income, because tenants tend to renew their leases. Like office leases, most industrial leases are written for long periods and are designed on the basis of *net rents*. Net rents require that tenants pay property taxes, insurance, and maintenance costs in addition to a base rent.

Shopping Centers

Conventional wisdom used to suggest that ownership of shopping centers involves little personal management and relatively high, risk-free yields. After all, with a K-Mart as an anchor store, what could possibly go wrong? K-Mart's bankruptcy, as well as those of a host of well-known department stores over the 1980s and 1990s, reveals that shopping center investment is not necessarily risk-free. Many older shopping malls have lost retailers to newer shopping malls as well.

Strip Store Buildings

In many towns and cities, small shopping plazas serve neighborhoods with a variety of local services and products. Their appeal to the investor is that most tenants are long-term (three to five years) and are likely to renew their leases because they establish a clientele at that location. They also tend to take care of their properties and expect the landlord to do the same.

Neighborhood Shopping Centers

The neighborhood center typically has a supermarket or drug-discount store as its anchor, often occupying around 30 percent to 40 percent of the total space available. They are located at major intersections near residential areas and transportation arteries because most shopping trips start at home. It's not uncommon for landlords to shift most or all of the maintenance costs to the tenants.

Regional Shopping Malls

Regional shopping malls favor locations near expressways and interstate highways. The regional shopping center developer may look for tracts of land that are larger than needed in order to profit from the increase in surrounding land value as a result of development.

Retail sales are greater in areas that have nearby competition, even when it is direct competition in terms of merchandise, prices, quality, and brands. This accounts for the common practice of a shopping center having several anchor tenants that are in direct competition. Functionally different businesses also help each other. Businesses such as department stores, furniture stores, and car dealers serve a *generative function*—that is, they generate business from shoppers who *intend* to go there. Businesses such as ice-cream shops and flower shops serve a *suscipient function*—that is, their business depends on attracting passersby.

Shopping center leases are likely to contain clauses allowing landlords to participate in gross sales. Landlords typically charge 1 percent to 4 percent of gross sales over a certain amount. Sometimes these leases are referred to as *percentage leases.*

Over the past five years, landlords of older shopping malls have added entertainment corridors (movie theaters, video game arcades) and food courts, and many have done major renovations and updating. This trend attracts patrons and drives sales up, thereby enhancing the landlords' revenues as well.

Security issues such as handling security emergencies and maintaining decorum have also been relatively new developments. For this reason and others, professional property management of shopping centers is a must.

The events of September 11, 2001, focused attention on the importance of building and property security. Florida property managers discovered that terrorists had rented several Florida apartments and used them to congregate and plan. Concerns have also been voiced about the possibility of rented property being used to warehouse and conceal dangerous chemicals and explosives.

The National Multi Housing Council (NMHC) has produced a guidance document for apartment owners and managers to help them respond to heightened security concerns. This document outlines procedures that property managers can use to supervise and monitor tenants and property, such as inspecting property routinely and closely interviewing prospective tenants. Other recommended steps are detailed in the document. The free guidance memo for apartment owners is posted on NMHC's Web site at *www.nmhc.org/Content/ServeContent.cfm?ContentItemID=2489.*

Commercial property managers are also advised to increase security, including adding access controls, alarms, closed-circuit cable TV monitoring, patrols, staff awareness training, policies and procedures, contingency plans, perimeter fortifications, and window glazing and other fortification.

■ Industrial Properties

Industrial properties provide places where manufacturing, processing, assembly, warehousing, and distribution can take place. Location is important for industrial properties, but the considerations involved are different from those for other types of property. High-volume traffic locations are important to retail sales but not to industrial buildings. Expressways, railroads, and rivers are important for industrial properties, but they may have less significance or even be negative features for other uses.

Industries engaged in obtaining or processing raw materials *(weight-reducing operations)* will favor locations close to the source of the raw materials. An example of a weight-reducing operation is a potassium mining business. Industries requiring material that is readily available *(weight-gaining operations)* will favor locations close to market areas to facilitate distribution. An example of a weight-gaining operation is a soft-drink bottling facility that needs to add water to its syrup product.

Like office leases, most industrial leases are written for long periods and are designed on the basis of *net rents*. Net rents require that tenants pay property taxes, insurance, and maintenance costs in addition to a base rent.

■ Specialty Investments

There are numerous possibilities for those who wish to invest in specialized real estate: mobile-home parks, hotels and motels, amusement parks, and golf courses, just to name a few. Another relatively new area of investment is adult congregate living facilities (ACLF) for older adults. What was once a relatively small area of real estate investment has now become a multibillion-dollar investment arena.

Many of these properties have grown in popularity because of the increase in leisure time available today. Older adults no longer wish to maintain lawns or worry about other maintenance problems. They also want convenience. Developing specialty properties often incurs high front-end costs and involves long-term expensive marketing. Specialty properties require special skills and knowledge to ensure the owner's success.

Because local zoning issues have to be addressed, specialized real estate investment projects often involve a significant amount of planning time.

■ Qualifying the Investor

Matching the investor with the right property involves knowing and considering the buyer's financial and personality profiles.

While it is important to review the purchase price of the property, it is the rare investor who pays cash for the investment. It is much more important, therefore, to look at other financial considerations.

Amount of Initial Investment Required

In addition to funds the investor must have for a down payment (usually 20 percent to 25 percent of the purchase price), the investor also needs cash for closing costs. Closing costs can easily run another 2 percent to 4 percent of the purchase price. In addition, the property may need a cash infusion for repairs and improvements. The investor may need additional monies to cover negative cash flow, which is likely for the first six months to several years of owning an investment property.

Amount and Timing of Cash Flows Expected from the Investment

Investors will articulate their needs to have their investment start to support itself. They will have goals in terms of *when* the investment should start to reap positive cash flow and *how much* cash flow they expect. Real estate professionals should be prepared to hear unsophisticated or naive landlords' unrealistic expectations regarding both goals and to counsel their clients appropriately. While it is possible to speed up the timetable for achieving positive cash flow, this is often accomplished if landlords provide a larger down payment and take a corresponding smaller loan with lower debt service.

Ability to Sell the Investment Quickly and at Full Price

Real estate practitioners should ask their landlord-clients about the timing of the sale of the investment. This information will be helpful in choosing the appropriate property. For example, as mentioned earlier, single-family homes are much easier to sell than multifamily homes. If a client expresses the need to sell the investment in five years, it might be wiser to suggest investing in a single-family home than in a large apartment complex. By the same token, should an investor consider a longer timetable, say 10 to 20 years, a large apartment complex or shopping center might be suitable. Investors should be reminded that real estate is largely an illiquid asset and can rarely be sold quickly at full price. Investors with a longer timetable for performance will likely be happier clients.

The Certainty of Anticipated Investment Performance

Some investors want to be certain that they will achieve their investment goals, whatever they may be. But real estate professionals should be wary of expressing any such certainty about the future, particularly for clients who may be holding on to properties for a very long time. Who knows how tax laws or the economy might change, even in the next year, not to mention five or ten years from now?

If investors indicate that they need to average 10 percent per year up to the time of sale so they can achieve their goal of retirement or sending Junior to Yale, they should be advised that real estate investment, while likely to appreciate, cannot offer guarantees. Investors with unrealistic expectations about returns on investments should be advised appropriately.

Amount of Expertise and Time Required to Manage the Investment

One of the most important questions that real estate licensees can ask investors is, "Do you have the time and expertise to manage your investment?" As mentioned earlier, maintaining rental property is both labor- and time-intensive. Some landlords enjoy fixing property up and being personally involved in their investments. They may have spare time available. They may also have past investment experience and expertise.

However, if clients are unskilled in or unprepared for dealing with tenant and property problems, they should be advised to seek professional property management. (Many real estate firms wisely offer this service to prospective landlords.) It is quite possible that clients may plan to be absentee landlords, and they also will need property management.

Yield Measurement

One gauge of investor sophistication is the yield measurement being used. When real estate professionals ask, "What kind of return on investment are you expecting?" they receive all kinds of responses in terms of percentages and types of returns.

When a prospective landlord states "a 5 percent return," the real estate agent needs to know if the client is referring to

- a 5 percent return on a cash investment equal to the purchase price (capitalization rate);

- a 5 percent return on the down payment (equity dividend rate);

- a 5 percent return on the down payment, closing costs, and other initial expenses;

- a before-tax 5 percent return;

- an after-tax 5 percent return;

- a 5 percent return this year;

- an average 5 percent return for every year of ownership; or

- a 5 percent return including sale proceeds (financial management rate of return).

In other words, it is important that real estate agents and their clients agree on the terminology and type of yield measurement used to define investment goals. Some of these yield measurements are basic; others are much more sophisticated. (In subsequent chapters, we are going to examine each of these yield measurements.)

Motivation to Reduce Taxes

In previous decades, particularly the 1980s, affluent investors chose real estate as a vehicle to shelter their primary sources of income from taxes. Many of them chose real estate properties that were not particularly financially sound, reasoning that they did not need more income. What they needed was to shelter the other income they were earning. Real estate fulfilled that purpose until 1987 when tax laws changed, eliminating many tax-sheltering qualities of real estate.

Affluent investors realized that real estate was no longer sheltering their primary income, and if the real property did not provide any income, there was no reason to keep the investment. Many investment properties—big downtown office buildings and large apartment buildings—were sold at distressed prices in the aftermath of tax reform.

Sophisticated real property investors realize that healthy real estate investment should do both: shelter primary income from tax and shelter its own income. Real estate licensees should ask wannabe-investors how critical the tax-sheltering qualities of their investment will be. They should also counsel their investors to make any offer or contract on property subject to the review of their tax advisers.

Pride of Ownership

For some investors, it is important to be able to point to their investments and say to their friends, "See that building? I own it. It's mine." These investors are concerned about prestige, perhaps even more than yield. Investors who want pretty buildings must be prepared to sacrifice some yield because keeping buildings pretty costs money. The inverse is also true: ugly buildings have higher yields. Slumlords don't invest a lot of money in upkeep and improvement and therefore achieve stunning rates of return. Ideally, real estate agents would not have potential slumlords as clients and would caution clients that to maintain *long-term* value of the building, landlords *must reinvest* in the building's upkeep.

Geographic Stability

Some investors know they are going to remain in an area for a long time. However, some investors know that their primary job may cause them to be reassigned to another location. Geographic stability can be a major factor in determining what investment is appropriate. It is challenging to be a long-distance owner of real estate, particularly if it is residential real estate.

Some investors know at the point of the investment search that they will not be staying in the area. In many college towns, parents buy duplexes for their college-age son or daughter and hope that their offspring will be able to maintain it for a few years.

When clients indicate that their future may be geographically unstable, it is appropriate to advise them to consider professional property management.

Desire to Maximize Future Wealth

It is unfortunate that so many real estate bestsellers and television ads have convinced would-be real estate investors that it is highly probable that with a minimum down payment, anyone can make a million dollars in real estate overnight. While undoubtedly there are some cases of investors turning a quick profit, most wealth from real estate is *not* created in the short term. Some real estate practitioners should consider working with only those investors who are seeking to maximize their future wealth and are willing to hold their investments for several years—if not for longer.

Tax laws favor long-term wealth building. The best capital gains tax breaks accrue to those investors who hold their assets for at least one year. Tax laws permit investors to hold on to their properties forever and then, on their death, pass them on to their heirs. Their heirs may pay no capital gains tax if they sell those properties shortly after receiving their inheritance for a price equal to the properties' value at the time of the inheritance.

Selling real estate investments held for a long time could invoke a large capital gains tax under many circumstances, but *exchanging* investment property can result in the indefinite postponement of capital gains taxes. One of the yield measurement tools used in this text, the financial management rate of return, focuses on long-term wealth building.

■ Summary

Qualifying an investor is a different process from qualifying a prospective homebuyer. Not only must real estate professionals ask the right questions, they must also provide advice on the appropriate investment property. Investment property considerations should include, among other issues, types of investment property. Investors can choose among residential properties, office buildings, shopping centers, industrial properties, and specialty investments. Each type of property has its own unique characteristics as well as advantages and disadvantages.

Matching the investor with the right property involves knowing and considering the buyer's financial and personality profiles. Real estate professionals should qualify investors based on such financial considerations as the investor's amount of initial investment required, the amount and timing of cash flows expected from the investment, the investor's expertise and time required to manage the investment, the yield measurement being used, the investor's motivation to reduce taxes, desire for pride of ownership, need to reduce taxes, and desire to maximize future wealth.

■ Chapter 4 Review Questions

1. Investment property considerations should include all of the following EXCEPT
   a. purchase price and terms.
   b. available financing.
   c. cash flows, positive or negative.
   d. commuting time from work.

2. Which of the following statements regarding fair housing laws is NOT true?
   a. Federal, state, and local fair housing laws are designed to eliminate discrimination in the sale or rental of housing because of race, color, religion, sex, national origin, handicap, or familial status.
   b. There are some limited exemptions for some landlords regarding discrimination under federal fair housing.
   c. Local fair housing laws may be even stricter than federal or state laws.
   d. Landlords cannot be fined or jailed for violating fair housing laws.

3. The terms *generative* and *suscipient function* are related to
   a. industrial property.
   b. shopping centers.
   c. residential properties.
   d. office properties.

4. The neighborhood center typically has a supermarket or drug-discount store as its anchor, often occupying around what percentage of the total space available?
   a. 10% – 25%
   b. 20% – 30%
   c. 30% – 40%
   d. 100%

5. If clients are unskilled or unprepared for dealing with tenant and property problems, they should be advised to
   a. avoid investing in real estate.
   b. seek professional property management.
   c. seek legal advice.
   d. seek accounting advice.

6. Which of the following may govern a residential dwelling unit used for rental purposes?
   a. State landlord-tenant laws
   b. Fair housing laws
   c. Building codes
   d. All of the above

7. A net lease requires that a tenant will pay for all of the following EXCEPT
   a. property taxes.
   b. insurance.
   c. improvements.
   d. maintenance.

8. A mining operation is an example of a
   a. generative function.
   b. suscipient function.
   c. weight-gaining operations.
   d. weight-reducing operations.

9. Clients who desire attractive properties may have to sacrifice
   a. amount and timing of cash flows.
   b. geographic stability.
   c. prestige.
   d. yield.

10. When a client responds to questions about anticipated performance of an investment by stating "I want a 10 percent return," the real estate practitioner should
    a. determine what yield measurement the client is using.
    b. determine if the desired return is realistic.
    c. counsel the client if the desired return is unrealistic.
    d. All of the above

Yield Measurements

learning objectives

After completing this chapter, you will be able to

■ describe and calculate yield using the capitalization rate measurement;

■ evaluate the advantages and disadvantages of the capitalization rate yield measurement;

■ calculate before-tax cash flow;

■ describe and calculate yield using the cash-on-cash measurement;

■ evaluate the advantages and disadvantages of the cash-on-cash return yield measurement; and

■ appropriately apply the terms *pro forma* and *reconstructed operating statement*.

■ Key Terms

before-tax cash flow	effective gross income	potential gross income
capitalization	equity dividend rate	reserve for replacements
cash-on-cash return	fixed expenses	vacancy and collection
contract rent	market rent	losses
debt service	net operating income	variable expense

■ Introduction

Investors desire the maximum rate of return for each dollar invested. The investment's yield should reflect the risk associated with the investment. In other words, riskier ventures should have correspondingly higher yields than a low-risk investment.

Yields comprise the return *of* the investment as well as the return *on* the investment during the holding period. As mentioned earlier, investors use a variety of different methods to measure yield. In this chapter we look at two yield measurements: capitalization rate and the cash-on-cash return (equity dividend rate). In later chapters, we look at one more yield measure: the financial management rate of return (FMRR). Each yield tool has advantages and disadvantages.

■ Capitalization Rate

Real estate students typically encounter the terms *cap rate* and *IRV* (income ÷ rate = value) when they study appraisal or valuation in prelicensing courses. The assumption that underlies the use of cap rates in appraisals is that *buyers will pay cash for their investment.* When real estate practitioners or investors use capitalization or cap rates to measure an investment's return, they are also making the assumption that an investment's return will be based on a cash investment; in other words, there will be no use of leveraging in the transaction. The unlikely scenario of investors paying all cash for an investment is one of the reasons that capitalization rates, while appropriate yield measurements for appraisal projects, are considered a fairly primitive or basic yield measurement tool for investors.

Arriving at the Cap Rate

Capitalization is defined as the process of converting future income into a single present value amount. Each time an investment property sells it produces a capitalization or "cap" rate. If there are enough sales of investment properties within a given market area, appraisers can "extract" a cap rate from the marketplace.

The formula for deriving the cap rate is

Net Operating Income ÷ Sales Price or Value = Capitalization Rate or NOI ÷ V = R

Here's an example of how this formula can be applied: Assume that an investment property sold for $750,000 and that it had a net operating income (NOI) of $75,000:

> $75,000 Net Operating Income ÷ $750,000 Sales Price or Value
> = .10 Capitalization Rate

Appraisers will use several investment property sales to derive an average or overall cap rate for use in their appraisal. If appraisers do not have enough sales to arrive at an average cap rate, they may use current market conditions and investors' expectations to arrive at an appropriate but more complex capitalization rate.

Current market conditions refer to the current lending terms and conditions set by lending institutions. For example, current commercial loans may be at 7.5 percent with 25 percent down and a term of 15 years. This varies from time to time, market to market, and lender to lender. Thus, one aspect of the cap rate is lender-driven.

The second factor is investor-driven. When investors decide to invest their money, they weigh the risk involved against the potential profit to be made. The higher the risk, the more profit is typically expected. Each investor sets individual expectations based on such issues as knowledge, experience, and tolerance for risk. The important point is that each investor sets parameters that will affect the cap rate. A cap rate may be a blend of current lender expectations with the expectations of each unique investor.

Review the following example:

Determining Cap Rate

Ms. Jackson wishes to purchase a business that is currently being offered for sale for $1,000,000. The best financing that she can obtain in the area calls for 25 percent down with the balance of 75 percent to be financed over a 15-year period at a rate of 9 percent interest. She has considered other possible ways to invest $250,000, but the yield (return on her investment) is currently quite low. Her expectation is, given the potential risk of the investment, a yield of 8 percent on her down payment over the holding period of the loan for this investment.

Down payment	$250,000 (lender-driven)
Expected yield	8% (investor-driven)
Lender loan	$750,000 (lender-driven)
Interest rate	9% (lender-driven)
Term	15 yrs. (lender-driven)

$$.75 \text{ (\% of loan made by lender)} \times .09 \text{ (interest rate)} = 0.0675$$
$$.25 \text{ (down payment)} \times .08 \text{ (yield expected)} = \underline{0.0200}$$
$$\text{Capitalization rate} \quad 0.0875$$

This cap rate of 8.75 percent would return 8 percent interest to the investor and 9 percent interest to the lender. However, lenders expect more than an interest-only payment, so a more accurate calculation of cap rate would have to include a factor for return of principal as well. The cap rate could be further adjusted so that the investor would recapture his or her initial investment over the life of the loan, much as the lending institution does. For simplicity's sake, we will assume that there are enough similar investment properties available to derive an overall cap rate rather than to use more elaborate market- and investor-derived capitalization rates.

Arriving at Net Operating Income (NOI)

To estimate the value of investment property to a cash investor using cap rates, real estate professionals must obtain the income and expense statement of the current property owner. It would be preferable for the current owner to have at least two years of operating statements so that projections of income and expenses can be inferred. In many cases, landlord/owners do not keep good records.

Real estate practitioners should create a projected income and expenses statement known as a *pro forma*. A pro forma is a projection of income and expenses for the next 12 months based on trends of the previous one or two years and data from other available resources. A pro forma is essentially a reconstruction of the previous years' income and expense statements and is sometimes referred to as a *reconstructed operating statement*.

Because the pro forma is developed for a 12-month period, the figures provided are always annual figures. Review the following example of a simple pro forma:

Determining Net Operating Income	
Potential gross income (PGI) (2 units at 550 monthly)	$13,200
– Vacancies (5%)	– 660
Effective gross income	$12,540
– Operating expenses	– 3,700
Net operating income	$ 8,840

Potential gross income (PGI) is the total annual income the property will produce if fully rented. If the current owner has tenants who have signed long-term leases, then the stipulated *contract rent* is used to determine PGI. If the units are likely to be vacant during the next 12 months, then real estate professionals must estimate what the *market rent* will be by finding comparable rental units and determining their market value.

Effective gross income (EGI) is the total annual income that is actually expected to be received. This is the potential gross income minus any vacancy and collection losses. *Vacancy and collection losses* are estimated based on typical management experience, not the current owner's experience. The current owner may reside on the property, causing vacancy and collection losses to be higher or lower than normal. (Estimates for vacancies can often be obtained from city and/or county building offices that issue building permits, from local real estate reports published by newspapers, or from real estate market analysts who may work independently or for real estate development or consulting firms.) Collection losses are expenses related to evictions and other rent collection problems.

Net operating income (NOI) is the total annual income after paying all operating expenses. This is the effective gross income minus operating expenses. There are three types of operating expenses: fixed, variable, and reserve for replacements.

1. *Fixed expenses* are those operating expenses that must be paid whether a property is occupied or not, such as real estate taxes and insurance.
2. *Variable expenses* are those expenses related to the actual operations of the property, such as utilities and maintenance.
3. *Reserve for replacements* is an annual reserve established for the replacement of items that wear out from time to time, such as air-conditioners and heating systems.

All of these expenses can be estimated either by reviewing the last two years of expenses and then projecting by how much these expenses will increase (or decrease) over the next 12 months or by contacting resources having this information. For example, real estate practitioners can call the property tax office to estimate what property taxes will be over the next year. They can contact the current owner's insurance agent to find out what increases in insurance premiums may occur. *Debt service* or *mortgage payments* are *not* considered operating expenses because they are not standard expense items but instead will vary from one potential owner to the next, depending on the terms of the transaction.

Further, the assumption of this yield measurement is that the investor will pay cash; therefore, there will be no debt service. The same is true of *tax depreciation*, which is an ownership expense, not an operating expense. Depreciation is *not* an operating expense.

Using the previously described example, if the NOI is $8,840 and the cap rate derived from comparable investments is 10 percent, a cash investor should be willing to pay $88,400, or

$$\$8,840 \text{ NOI} \div 10\% \text{ R}_{CAP} = \$88,400 \text{ Value}$$

Advantages and Disadvantages of Capitalization Rates

Capitalization rates provide a relatively simple tool for estimated value of an investment to a cash investor. Using this yield measurement, investors and their agents must review and consider the impact of operating expenses on the value of the investment. They must also discuss the very real possibility of periodic vacancies and collection problems. The development of a pro forma can be an important exercise and an opportunity to discuss the expenses involved in owning investment real estate.

Unfortunately, this method does have shortcomings. For one, this type of pro forma requires only a 12-month projection of income and expenses. The majority of investor clients will hold their investments longer and thus need to consider how income and expenses will change over time. More seriously, the capitalization method requires that agents and clients assume that the transaction will be 100 percent cash. This is unlikely. Thus, this model of valuation does not take into account the impact of leveraging the transaction. The impact of leverage, as discussed in Chapter 1 and further explained in this chapter, can be significant.

Another shortcoming of this method is that appreciation is not factored into the value of the property—not even for the 12-month projection. Neither the impact of paying taxes on the income generated by the building nor the impact of paying capital gains tax on the proceeds from the sale is considered.

Thus, the capitalization rate method, while valuable to appraisers, proves to be a rather limited investment yield measurement.

■ Cash-on-Cash Return (Equity Dividend Rate)

Another yield measurement corrects for some of the deficiencies found in the capitalization rate method. The *cash-on-cash return*, sometimes referred to as the *equity dividend rate* or *ratio* (EDR), measures the return received on the initial investment in the property. This yield measurement assumes that the investor does not pay cash for the investment property but rather leverages the transaction. Thus, a more realistic review of the property would be to consider the return on the initial investment or down payment rather than on the cash price of the investment.

The formula for the cash-on-cash return is

Before-Tax Cash Flow ÷ Amount of Equity = Cash-on-Cash Return (EDR)

Review the following example:

Mr. and Mrs. Ott have decided to purchase an investment property based on the pro forma described earlier. It is a residential condominium apartment. The Otts are going to finance the purchase of this investment by borrowing $85,000 at 8.5 percent over 30 years. The debt service (principal and interest) or mortgage payments will be approximately $652 monthly or $7,825 yearly, of which an approximate $600 is principal reduction in the first year. (The amount of principal reduction becomes important in later calculations of after-tax cash flow.)

The Otts' before-tax cash flow (BTCF) on this property is calculated as follows:

Projected gross income	$13,200
– Vacancies (5%)	– 660
Effective gross income	$12,540
– Operating expenses	– 3,700
Net operating income	$ 8,840
– Debt service (assume $600 is principal)	– 7,825
Before-tax cash flow (BTCF)	$ 1,015

Notice that this calculation is similar to the pro forma created in the discussion of capitalization rates. The difference here is that the real estate practitioner and investor have considered the impact of borrowing—in this case $85,000 at 8.5 percent. Thus an additional expense would be the debt service (mortgage payments) on the loan, an estimated $7,825 (including $600 of principal reduction). The investor would be left with *before-tax cash flow* of $1,015.

Before-tax cash flow (BTCF) is also called *cash throwoff* or *pre-tax cash flow*. It is hoped that a real estate investment will generate positive pre-tax cash flow. The before-tax cash flow is a before-tax measurement of cash generated by the property. The formula is

Net Operating Income – Debt Service = Before-Tax Cash Flow

Once the before-tax cash flow is known, the cash-on-cash return (or EDR) can be calculated. Again, this is the rate of return to the equity investment generated annually by the property. The formula is

Before-Tax Cash Flow ÷ Amount of Equity = Cash-on-Cash Return (or EDR)

Review the following example:

$$\frac{\$1,015 \ BTCF}{\$15,000 \ Down \ Payment} = 6.8\% \ Cash\text{-}on\text{-}Cash \ Return \ (or \ EDR)$$

Some investors and real estate agents prefer to calculate the cash-on-cash return on the entire initial investment—the down payment plus the closing costs. In the example above, if closing costs were $3,000, then the calculation would be

$$\frac{\$1,015 \text{ BTCF}}{\$18,000 \ (\$15,000 \text{ Down Payment} + \$3,000 \text{ Costs})} = 5.6\% \text{ Cash-on-Cash Return (EDR)}$$

Is a 5 percent to 6 percent return on investment an acceptable rate? That depends on the investor's desired goals and expectations. Certainly, in the heyday of the '90s stock market, a return of 5 percent to 6 percent would have looked paltry compared with the 20 percent returns on various high-tech stocks. In the aftermath of the stock market decline, a 5 percent to 6 percent return looks pretty good! But again, the investor has to compare these returns with other possible investment alternatives and consider all of the possible risk factors.

Advantages and Disadvantages of the Cash-on-Cash Return Yield Measurement

The clear advantage of this measurement tool is that, unlike the capitalization rate method, the cash-on-cash return measurement takes into account the effect of financing: the impact of mortgage payments is considered in the calculation.

However, this yield measurement still looks at only one year's worth of ownership. Because it does not take into account the possibility of a long-term ownership position, it ignores appreciation, as does the capitalization rate method. It also fails to take into account the tax consequences of ownership—not only on the income derived from the property on an annual basis but also on the capital gains tax on the proceeds from the sale.

■ Summary

Investors use a variety of different methods to measure yield. In this chapter, we looked at two yield measurements: the capitalization rate and the cash-on-cash return (equity dividend rate). Each yield tool has advantages and disadvantages.

Capitalization rates are often used by appraisers to estimate the present cash value of small investment properties. Practitioners who use capitalization rates assume the investor will pay cash and not borrow any funds for the purchase. The capitalization rate is used in conjunction with projected income and expense statements, known as *pro formas*, that are based on a one-year projection. The net operating income represents the "bottom line" of the pro forma and is divided by a market-derived capitalization rate to obtain the present value of the investment. However, pro formas do not take into account longer investment periods nor do they consider the impact of long-term appreciation or tax consequences of owning or selling investment property. Thus, the capitalization rate method is somewhat primitive.

The measurement known as the *cash-on-cash return*, in contrast, considers the impact of borrowing on the investment's yield. Debt service or mortgage payments are used to derive before-tax cash flow, which is then divided by the actual equity investment to derive the cash-on-cash return. However, this yield measurement still looks at only one year's worth of ownership. Because it does not take into account the possibility of a long-term ownership position, it ignores appreciation, as does the capitalization rate method. It also fails to take into account the tax consequences of ownership.

In the next chapter, we will consider a more sophisticated method of yield measurement that will take these problems into consideration.

■ Chapter 5 Review Questions

1. The formula for deriving the cap rate is
   - **a.** net operating income ÷ value.
   - **b.** value ÷ net operating income.
   - **c.** before-tax cash flow ÷ down payment.
   - **d.** down payment ÷ before-tax cash flow.

2. Real estate practitioners should create a projected income and expenses statement known as a
   - **a.** reconstructed operating statement.
   - **b.** pro forma.
   - **c.** Neither a nor b
   - **d.** Both a and b

3. The *cash-on-cash return* is sometimes referred to as the
   - **a.** capitalization rate.
   - **b.** pro forma rate.
   - **c.** equity dividend rate.
   - **d.** T-bill rate.

4. A commercial property recently sold for $528,000, and it has a net operating income of $79,200 per year. What is the rate of return (capitalization rate)?
   - **a.** 6.67%
   - **b.** 14.90%
   - **c.** 14.95%
   - **d.** 15%

5. An investor wishes to purchase a $250,000 warehouse with 20 percent down. She expects that the net operating income will be $25,000 and debt service will be $18,000. What is the anticipated cash-on-cash return rate?
   - **a.** 10%
   - **b.** 12.5%
   - **c.** 14%
   - **d.** 20%

6. Real estate taxes are an example of
   - **a.** fixed expenses.
   - **b.** variable expenses.
   - **c.** capital expenses.
   - **d.** reserves.

7. If a residential property has a net operating income of $49,200 per year and an appraiser uses a capitalization rate of 12 percent, the estimated property value is
   - **a.** $118,800.
   - **b.** $232,902.
   - **c.** $410,000.
   - **d.** $786,060.

8. A building has an annual net operating income of $10,500 with expenses averaging $2,500. Assuming a capitalization rate of 9 percent, what is the present cash value?
   - **a.** $88,888
   - **b.** $116,667
   - **c.** $144,444
   - **d.** $165,000

9. An apartment complex contains 30 units that each rent for $400 per month. Assuming a vacancy rate of 5 percent and annual operating expenses of $54,000, what would be the appraised value with a capitalization rate of 10 percent?
   - **a.** $828,000
   - **b.** $1,200,000
   - **c.** $1,368,000
   - **d.** $1,444,000

10. The advantage of the cash-on-cash measurement tool over the capitalization rate method is that the cash-on-cash return method
   - **a.** takes into account the effect of financing.
   - **b.** takes into account a long-term ownership position.
   - **c.** takes into account appreciation.
   - **d.** considers tax consequences.

6

Understanding the Financial Management Rate of Return

After completing this chapter, you will be able to

- discuss the advantages of the financial management rate of return (FMRR) yield measurement compared with other yield measurement tools;

- list the assumptions of the FMRR;

- appropriately apply the terms *depreciation* and *after-tax cash flow*;

- discuss the tax implications of real estate investments;

- calculate depreciation allowances under current tax laws; and

- calculate after-tax cash flow and taxable income.

■ Key Terms

active income	financial management rate of return (FMRR)	portfolio income
after-tax cash flow		positive taxable income
depreciation	negative taxable income	total acquisition cost
	passive income	

■ Introduction

The financial management rate of return (FMRR) is considered by many experts to be an excellent investment measurement tool (see Preface). In the previous chapter, the capitalization rate and the cash-on-cash return methods were discussed. Their limitations—the inability to calculate the impact of leveraging, appreciation, and tax consequences—can be overcome with the FMRR.

Unlike those who use the cap rate and cash-on-cash return, investors and licensees who use the FMRR yield measurement assume that investors want long-term wealth building. Thus, the impact of appreciation and after-tax consequences are taken into consideration. Financing, appreciation, and taxes are significant because their effect on the investment's income represents the investor's *real, spendable dollars*. The FMRR also takes into consideration positive and/or negative cash flows and their value or cost to the investor. This model makes it possible to compare the return on real estate with other liquid investment returns, providing a real "apples-to-apples" comparison.

To be able to calculate an investment's FMRR, it is necessary to understand several concepts, including the time value of money and taxes.

■ Fundamental Investment Attitudes toward Cash Flow

Experienced investors understand the *time value of money.* A good real estate investment produces periodic income over a long period of time. A good investment property also provides income at the end of the property's usefulness to the investor; hopefully, the property will produce an after-tax profit at its sale. The promise of those two sources of future income—periodic income and sales proceeds—has value today.

The assumptions of the FMRR are as follows:

- A small initial investment is better than a bigger one.
- Receiving cash sooner from an investment is better than receiving cash later.
- A larger periodic cash flow is better than a smaller one.
- Larger proceeds from a sale are better than smaller ones.

The first assumption regarding a small initial investment reflects the typical investor's desire to leverage the real estate transaction, risking less of the investors' funds and putting the risk on the lender.

The second assumption could be borrowed from one of Aesop's proverbs: "A bird in the hand is worth two in the bush." This expression means that it is better to have something tangible in your hand today than the promise of something tomorrow. The same applies to cash. Cash in the investor's hands today has a greater value than money that will be received tomorrow. The problem with future income is not only its unpredictability but also that future income can be devalued by inflation or deflation.

Having more income (a larger periodic cash flow or larger sales proceeds) is always worth more today and in the future than lesser cash flows.

How much value these sources of income provides depends on the individual investor's desired rates of return. Compound interest tables can help investors calculate the present value of future income. The FMRR requires the use of these tables several times in the calculation of the rate. (See discussion in Chapter 7.)

■ Calculating Taxable Income

Investors must report the income from their rental properties to the IRS and may owe tax on that income. To determine the potential tax bite, investors must know how to calculate taxable cash flow.

Review the following illustration of the Otts' planned purchase used in Chapter 5:

Projected gross income	$13,200
– Vacancies (5%)	– 660
Effective gross income	$12,540
– Operating expenses	– 3,700
Net operating income	$ 8,840
– Debt service (assume $600 is principal)	– 7,825
Before tax cash flow	$ 1,015

Now, to calculate taxable income, two other factors must be considered: (1) only the *interest* portion of debt service is tax deductible (not the principal) and (2) tax laws allow investors to take *depreciation* as a deduction as well.

The formula for calculating taxable income is

Net Operating Income – (Interest and Depreciation) = Taxable Income

Recall from the Otts' purchase that their debt service was $7,825. However, the majority of their debt service is interest. Only $600 (approximately) of their annual mortgage payment is attributable to principal. Thus, for tax purposes they may only use $7,225 of their mortgage payment ($7,825 – $600) in the calculation of taxable income.

Notice in the following example that when interest and depreciation are taken into account, it appears that the investment has actually *lost* income, not earned it.

Projected gross income	$13,200
– Vacancies	– 660
Effective gross income	$12,540
– Operating expenses	– 3,700
Net operating income	$ 8,840
– Interest ($600 principal)	– 7,225
– Depreciation	–10,815
Negative taxable income	– $ 9,200

Depreciation

The term *depreciation* refers to a building's loss in value. To appraisers, depreciation is an actual physical event. To a tax preparer, depreciation is a statutory allowance that symbolically represents the "wasting of an asset" and often has little bearing on the actual depreciation a building may experience.

To calculate the depreciation deduction, an investor should consider not only the purchase price of the property but also any closing costs associated with the acquisition of the property. Let's continue with the Otts' purchase. Assume that their investment choice is a condominium apartment they purchase for $100,000 plus $3,000 in closing costs. Their purchase price and closing costs total $103,000 (referred to as *total acquisition cost*). According to IRS regulations, the Otts may depreciate an appropriate percentage of the total acquisition cost that reflects the building's value out of the total value of the investment property. Review the following example:

Purchase price	$100,000
Closing costs	+ 3,000
Total acquisition costs	$103,000
Percent of building value	× 90%
Cost basis	$ 92,700

Note the use of 90 percent as the percentage of building value in this calculation. Because the Otts' investment is a condominium, it is entirely possible that 90 percent of the purchase price and closing costs can be attributed to the purchase of the building (and only 10 percent of the land). Remember that only buildings depreciate, *not* land. Should this investment property be a four-unit apartment building near the oceanfront, the investor would be hard-pressed to defend a 90 percent/10 percent split on the property and land. It might be more likely to be the other way around!

Investors should discuss the appropriate percentage to use with their legal and tax advisers and be prepared to defend their choice to the IRS. In an audit, it would be helpful to have (1) a sales contract that indicates what the investor paid for the building and the land separately, (2) an appraisal valuing the building and land separately, or (3) a tax assessment demonstrating the separate values of the building and the land.

Once the investor has calculated the cost basis of the building, he or she must then apply the appropriate depreciation allowance.

Changes in Depreciation Allowances

The depreciation allowances allowed by law have changed radically over the past 20-plus years.

1981 Depreciation Rules. If our investors, the Otts, purchased the very same condominium in 1981, tax laws at that time would have allowed them to write off their investment in 15 years.

1981 Depreciation Rules

$$\frac{\$92,700 \text{ Cost Basis}}{15 \text{ Years}} = \$6,180 \text{ Depreciation Allowance}$$

Further, under a depreciation system known as the modified accelerated cost recovery system (MACRS) that existed up until the Tax Reform Act of 1986, that allowance could have been multiplied by 175 percent, or

$$\$6,180 \times 175\% = \$10,815$$

Thus, in the example above, with the interest deduction of $7,226 and the depreciation allowance of $10,815, the building actually generates *negative taxable income* (net operating income – interest and depreciation = taxable income). Not only has this investment sheltered the $8,840 of net operating income it actually generated, the building is sheltering $9,200 of other income generated by the investor's other investment. In other words, this building is a *tax shelter*. A *tax shelter* is created when deductions exceed taxable income.

How much of an impact would this have on the 1981 investor? In 1981, the highest possible tax bracket was 50 percent. Review the following illustration of the tax consequences of owning this investment property for the 1981 investor.

1981 Tax Consequences of Investment Ownership

Projected gross income	$13,200
– Vacancies (5%)	– 660
Effective gross income	$12,540
– Operating expenses	– 3,700
Net operating income	$ 8,840
– Interest	– 7,225
– Depreciation	–10,815
Negative taxable income	– 9,200
Tax bracket	× 50%
Tax saved	$ 4,600

The 1981 investor would have a tax savings of $4,600, thanks to the tax-sheltering impact of this investment. In other words, *negative taxable cash flow created a positive tax savings*.

1985–1986 Depreciation Rules.   Unfortunately for real estate investors, tax laws changed dramatically in 1985. Depreciation allowances were reduced by increasing the depreciable life of buildings from 15 years to 18 years. Thus, if the Otts purchased this same condominium and put it in service in 1985 instead of 1981, the impact would have looked as follows:

1985 Depreciation Rules

$$\frac{\$92,700 \text{ Cost Basis}}{18 \text{ Years}} = \$5,150$$

$5,150 × 175% MACRS = $9,013 (Rounded) Depreciation Allowance

---

Review the consequences of the diminished depreciation allowance on the taxable income and resulting tax savings for the Otts.

1985 Tax Consequences of Investment Ownership

Projected gross income	$13,200
– Vacancies	– 660
Effective gross income	$12,540
– Operating expenses	– 3,700
Net operating income	$ 8,840
– Interest	– 7,225
– Depreciation	– 9,012
Negative taxable income	– 7,397
Tax bracket	× 50%
Tax saved	$ 3,699 (rounded)

Note that purchasing this condominium in 1985 under different tax rules would have reduced the depreciation allowance by more than $1,500, thereby diminishing the tax savings.

A technical modification to depreciation statutes took place in 1986, again reducing the possible benefit. Depreciation allowances were reduced by increasing the depreciable life of buildings from 18 years to 19 years.

1986 Depreciation Rules

$$\frac{\$92,700 \text{ Cost Basis}}{19 \text{ Years}} = \$4,879$$

$4,879 × 175% MACRS = $8,538 Depreciation Allowance

Note the impact of the change in depreciation allowance on the Otts' tax income and resulting tax savings.

1986 Tax Consequences of Investment Ownership	
Projected gross income	$13,200
– Vacancies	– 660
Effective gross income	$12,540
– Operating expenses	– 3,700
Net operating income	$ 8,840
– Interest	– 7,225
– Depreciation	– 8,538
Negative taxable income	– 6,923
Tax bracket	× 50%
Tax saved	$ 3,462

Again, note that if the same investment property had been put into service one year later, it would have meant a reduction in the possible tax savings.

Tax Reform Act of 1986. It was the subsequent Tax Reform Act of 1986 (TRA '86), however, that had the most significant impact on real estate investors. In addition to adding more years to the possible depreciable life of a building, thereby reducing the depreciation allowance, Congress took away MACRS. Unable to multiply their allowance by 175 percent, investors faced critically reduced amounts of depreciation deductions and suddenly found themselves with buildings that not only failed to shelter other investment income but also failed to shelter their own income. At the same time, Congress created different depreciation allowances for residential investments and commercial properties. Thus, if the Otts were to put their condominium investment property into service *today*, their depreciation allowance would be calculated as follows:

Residential Investment Property Today
$\dfrac{\$92,700 \text{ Cost Basis}}{27.5 \text{ Years}} = \$3,371$

If their investment were a commercial office condominium put into service today, their depreciation allowance would be calculated as follows:

Commercial Investment Property Today
$\dfrac{\$92,700 \text{ Cost Basis}}{39 \text{ Years}} = \$2,376$

Today's Tax Consequences of Investment Ownership

Additionally, in 2003, tax brackets were reduced. Unlike investors in the top tax bracket who paid 50 percent income tax, today's top-bracket taxpayers pay 35 percent. Thus, the example of the Otts' residential condominium investment put into service today would provide the following modest tax relief:

Projected gross income	$13,200
– Vacancies	– 660
Effective gross income	$12,540
– Operating expenses	– 3,700
Net operating income	$ 8,840
– Interest	– 7,225
– Depreciation	– 3,371
Negative taxable income	– 1,756
Tax bracket	× 35%
Tax *saved*	$ 615 (rounded)

Note that even with the more modest depreciation deduction of $3,371, this building still generates negative taxable income.

However, it is entirely possible that interest and depreciation allowances may not be large enough to offset net operating income, thereby creating *positive taxable* income and resulting taxes owed. Hypothetically, if, instead of the 8 percent financing used in the previous examples, the Otts had obtained 5 percent financing for 30 years (monthly mortgage payments of $456 or $5,472 annually with principal reduction in the first year of $1,247, approximately), the tax consequences of ownership might look as follows:

Projected gross income	$13,200
– Vacancies	– 660
Effective gross income	$12,540
– Operating expenses	– 3,700
Net operating income	$ 8,840
– Interest	– 4,225
– Depreciation	– 3,371
Positive taxable income	+ 1,244
Tax bracket	× 35%
Tax *owed*	$ 435 (rounded)

As a consequence of lower loan expenses, note that the Otts now *owe* taxes on their condominium investment's income.

■ Using the Tax Shelter

Current tax laws impose limits on how much negative taxable income a taxpayer can declare. Under TRA '86, taxpayers must classify their income as one of three types:

1. *active trade or business:* basically ordinary income, such as salaries and commissions

2. *portfolio activity:* interest, dividends, royalties, gains, or losses from sale of portfolio assets

3. *passive activity:* nonmaterial participation such as rental income, or income from limited partnerships

The most troublesome of the categories for real estate investors was the third, passive activity. Initially, the IRS classified most rental activity as passive income. This categorization became an issue when it was understood that under TRA '86, the IRS would allow taxpayers to write off losses based only on the category of income. In other words, a taxpayer could write off investment interest paid out on land (portfolio income) only if he or she had investment interest earned coming in (portfolio income). Investors could write off rental losses (passive activity) only if they had rental income (passive activity). The IRS indicated it wanted to see an "apples-to-apples" write-off.

Previously, the IRS had let investors write off passive losses against active trade or business income, creating the possibility of a true tax shelter. As might be imagined, this change was tremendously unpopular with real estate investors, who were no longer going to be allowed to write off huge losses against other income streams. Particularly hard hit were investors in very passive real estate investments, such as real estate investment trusts (REITs) and limited partnerships.

The IRS later relented, at least in regards to less-affluent investors. Under current tax laws, individuals who earn $100,000 or less (adjusted gross income) may, under some circumstances, write off their real estate losses. However, to qualify to do so, taxpayers must (1) actively manage their properties (or hire a manager) and (2) own at least 10 percent of the investment to qualify. If taxpayers meet these two tests, they are still limited to how much they can write off: up to $25,000 of real estate losses to offset other income—active or portfolio.

For the small real estate investors, then, current tax laws still allow the possibility of tax-sheltering investments. To reiterate, these investors must manage their own properties (or at least be involved in hiring a manager). If the total of their real estate income generates up to $25,000 of negative taxable income, they may write off all of those losses as long as they earn $100,000 or less.

Taxpayers who earn $100,000 to $150,000 are limited in their deductions. Those who make $150,000 or more are not permitted to deduct any rental property losses against active income. However, if taxpayers cannot write off all of their losses in a particular tax year, they may "bank" those losses until the time they sell their properties and use those losses to reduce their capital gains. Unfortunately, many affluent investors who wish to immediately use the tax-sheltering qualities of their real estate investments can no longer do so.

An exception to the earnings rules regarding writing off losses exists for real estate professionals. They can avoid the limits on rental real estate loss allowance if

- they are involved in real estate full-time or for 750 hours per year;
- they spend more than half of their time on real estate activities; and
- they manage their own properties (although daily chores can be delegated to a management company).

■ Calculating After-Tax Cash Flow

Once the taxable income has been determined, after-tax cash flow (ATCF) can be calculated. Review one more time the example discussed in Chapter 5 where the interest rate on the loan is 8 percent.

Projected gross income	$13,200
– Vacancies (5%)	– 660
Effective gross income	$12,540
– Operating expenses	– 3,700
Net operating income	$ 8,840
– Debt service (assume $600 is principal)	– 7,825
Before-tax cash flow	+ 1,015

Now review the analysis of the tax consequences of ownership today.

Projected gross income	$13,200
– Vacancies	– 660
Effective gross income	$12,540
– Operating expenses	– 3,700
Net operating income	$ 8,840
– Interest	– 7,225
– Depreciation	– 3,371
Negative taxable income	– 1,756
Tax bracket	× 35%
Tax saved	$ 615

Consider, then, how this condominium property has enhanced the Otts' return on this investment by calculating their ATCF.

The formula for calculating ATCF is

After-Tax Cash Flow (ATCF) = Before-Tax Cash Flow + Tax Saved (or – Tax Owed)

The ATCF on this building can be calculated as follows:

Before-tax cash flow	$1,015
+ Tax savings	+ 615
After-tax cash flow	$1,630

In other words, negative taxable income *increases* ATCF.

What if the same investment generated *positive* taxable income, as it does in the following example, where the interest is computed at 5 percent?

Projected gross income	$13,200
– Vacancies	– 660
Effective gross income	$12,540
– Operating expenses	– 3,700
Net operating income	$ 8,840
– Interest	– 4,225
– Depreciation	– 3,371
Positive taxable income	+ 1,244
Tax bracket	× 35%
Tax owed	$ 435

Positive taxable income *decreases* ATCF, as can be seen in the following example:

Before-tax cash flow	$1,015
– Tax savings	– 615
After-tax cash flow	$ 400

■ Summary

A good real estate investment produces periodic income over a long period of time. The FMRR can be used to estimate the current value of periodic income streams; however, for FMRR to be calculated, the investor must first calculate the investment's tax consequences.

Mortgage interest and depreciation can be deducted from net operating income to derive after-tax cash flow. The depreciation deduction is based on the building's acquisition costs and its statutory life (27.5 years for residential buildings; 39 years for commercial buildings). The depreciation allowance has diminished significantly over the past two decades.

Once the after-tax cash flow is known, the investor can determine the amount of taxes saved or owed. Under current tax laws, investors may be limited to the amount of negative taxable income that can be sheltered and used to save taxes.

Estimating after-tax cash flow is an important step in developing the financial management rate of return, as will be seen in the following chapters.

■ Chapter 6 Review Questions

1. The inability to calculate the impact of leveraging, appreciation, and tax consequences is overcome with what model of investment analysis?

   a. Equity dividend rate

   b. Capitalization rate

   c. Cash-on-cash return

   d. Financial management rate of return

2. Which is NOT an assumption of the FMRR?

   a. A bigger initial investment is better than a smaller one.

   b. Receiving cash sooner from an investment is better than receiving cash later.

   c. A larger periodic cash flow is better than a smaller one.

   d. A larger proceed from a sale is better than a smaller one.

3. To calculate taxable income, investors must know

   a. the net operating income.

   b. the interest portion of debt service.

   c. depreciation.

   d. All of the above

4. To a tax preparer, depreciation is all of the following EXCEPT

   a. a statutory allowance that symbolically represents the "wasting of an asset."

   b. the same as the actual depreciation a building may experience.

   c. a write-off against income.

   d. a tax allowance used on buildings, not land.

5. Over the years, tax laws have changed so that real estate investors have

   a. larger depreciation deductions.

   b. larger interest deductions.

   c. smaller depreciation deductions.

   d. more opportunities to create tax-sheltering real estate investments.

6. An investor who generates negative taxable income of $15,000 on real estate investments may write those losses off if the investor

   a. actively manages his or her properties or hires a manager.

   b. earns $100,000 or less adjusted gross income (AGI).

   c. owns at least 10 percent of the investment properties.

   d. All of the above

7. Tax laws today require that investors depreciate residential and commercial buildings over how many years, respectively?

   a. 10, 15

   b. 15, 30

   c. 18, 19

   d. 27.5, 39

8. Dividend and royalty income would be considered what kind of income by the IRS?

   a. Active trade or business

   b. Portfolio activity

   c. Passive activity

   d. Capital gains

9. Salaries and commissions would be considered what kind of income by the IRS?

   a. Active trade or business

   b. Portfolio activity

   c. Passive activity

   d. Capital gains

10. Income from limited partnerships and real estate investment trusts would be considered what kind of income by the IRS?

    a. Active trade or business

    b. Portfolio activity

    c. Passive activity

    d. Capital gains

The Time Value of Money

learning objectives

After completing this chapter, you will be able to

■ calculate the future value of an investment's lump sum income;

■ calculate the future value of an investment's annuity income;

■ calculate the present value of future income, whether in lump sum or in annuity;

■ calculate depreciation recapture; and

■ calculate the after-tax proceeds from the sale of a real estate investment.

■ Key Terms

acquisition cost	net after-tax sales proceeds	realized sales price
capital gain		

■ Introduction

In the previous chapter, the advantages of using the financial management rate of return (FMRR) were discussed. To determine the FMRR, real estate professionals and investors must be able to calculate taxable income as well as taxes saved or owed. This calculation was also discussed in the previous chapter.

Investors and licensees who use the FMRR assume that investors want long-term wealth building. Good real estate investment produces periodic income over a long period of time. A good investment property also provides income at the end of the property's usefulness to the investor; hopefully, the property will produce an after-tax profit at its sale. That promise of those two sources of future income—periodic income and sales proceeds—has value today. In this chapter, we are going to determine the value of those two sources of future income so that the FMRR can be calculated.

How much value these sources of income provide depends on the individual investor's desired rates of return. Compound interest Tables A and B at the end of this chapter can help investors calculate the present value of future income. The FMRR requires the use of these tables several times in the calculation of the rate.

■ Future Values of Lump Sums

Investments provide "lump sums" of cash as well as periodic returns. Some examples of lump sums in real estate would be the after-tax proceeds of the sale that the investor receives years from now or the initial funds (e.g., down payment and closing costs) invested in the property today. (See discussion later in this chapter.)

Problem A. Let's consider an easier example first. Assume that Jennifer, an investor, saves $1 every year and places it in a bank certificate of deposit (CD). Jennifer never adds another dollar to the initial $1 saved. Let's further assume that Jennifer will receive 10 percent interest on that $1 every year for ten years. How much would Jennifer's initial investment be worth ten years from now?

Solution. There are three ways to calculate the answer to this problem.

Method 1. Multiply the initial investment by the interest rate and add the earnings to the initial amount. Repeat by multiplying the total earnings by the interest rate and add the earnings to the new amount. Repeat for each of the ten years.

$1.00 × 10% = .10	$1.00 + .10 = $1.10 End of yr. 1
$1.10 × 10% = .11	$1.10 + .11 = $1.21 End of yr. 2
$1.21 × 10% = .12	$1.21 + .12 = $1.33 End of yr. 3
$1.33 × 10% = .13	$1.33 + .13 = $1.46 End of yr. 4
$1.46 × 10% = .15	$1.46 + .15 = $1.61 End of yr. 5
$1.61 × 10% = .16	$1.61 + .16 = $1.77 End of yr. 6
$1.77 × 10% = .18	$1.77 + .18 = $1.95 End of yr. 7
$1.95 × 10% = .20	$1.95 + .20 = $2.15 End of yr. 8
$2.15 × 10% = .22	$2.15 + .22 = $2.37 End of yr. 9
$2.37 × 10% = .24	$2.37 + .24 = $2.61 End of yr. 10

Method 2. Multiply the initial investment by 100 percent + interest rate. Repeat for each of the ten years.

$1.00		$1.61	
× 110%		× 110%	
$1.10	End of yr. 1	$1.77	End of yr. 6
× 110%		× 110%	
$1.21	End of yr. 2	$1.95	End of yr. 7
× 110%		× 110%	
$1.33	End of yr. 3	$2.15	End of yr. 8
× 110%		× 110%	
$1.46	End of yr. 4	$2.36	End of yr. 9
× 110%		× 110%	
$1.61	End of yr. 5	$2.60	End of yr. 10

Method 3. Use the compound interest table and find the appropriate factor for the interest rate and term. Multiply the initial investment by the factor.

Use Table A (see page 68) to look up the factor for 10 percent return for ten years. Note that the factor is 2.59. Multiply the lump sum of $1 by 2.59 = $2.59. Much simpler! In other words, the lump sum table reveals what the future value is of $1.

Problem B.   Here's another problem. Calculate the future value of $10,000 at 10 percent in ten years using Table A.

$10,000 × 2.594 = $25,940

Problem C.   Now, calculate the future value of $10,000 at 10 percent for 20 years using Table A.

$10,000 × 6.727 = $67,270

These calculations demonstrate the use of Table A to determine the *future value* of present income.

■ Present Value of Future Income Computed Using Table A

Another way to use Table A is to consider the *present value* of future income. Using the last problem, consider an investor's desire to have $67,270 saved over a 20-year period in an investment that yields 10 percent. By using Table A, we can calculate that the investor will have to invest $10,000 today in order to meet that goal.

$$\frac{\$67,270 \div 6.727}{\text{future value}} = \frac{\$10,000}{\text{present value}}$$

This type of calculation will be used in the FMRR to determine what projected after-tax proceeds from the sale of real estate are worth today.

■ Future Value of Annuity Income

Sometimes, investors place an annuity amount into an investment; that is, they regularly add to the investment every year. For example, traditional and Roth IRA investors place $2,000 per year (and sometimes more per year depending on the age of the investor) into their accounts. This sum of money is not a lump sum; rather, it is an annuity. Table B helps calculate the value of $1 today plus another $1 added.

Problem A. Let's assume that Jennifer is able to save more money than in the previous example. This time, Jennifer saves $1 in a bank savings account today and adds another dollar to the account every year. Let's further assume that Jennifer will receive 10 percent interest on that $1 each and every year for ten years. How much would Jennifer's initial investment be worth ten years from now?

Solution. There are three ways to calculate the answer to this problem.

Method 1. Multiply the initial investment by the interest rate and add the earnings to the initial amount. Add the amount of the initial investment to the new sum. Repeat by multiplying the total sum by the interest rate and add the earnings to the new amount. Repeat for each of the ten years.

$1.00 × 10% = .10	$1.00 + .10 = $1.10 End of yr. 1
$1.10 + 1.00 End of yr. 2 = $2.10 × 10% = .21	$2.10 + .21= $2.31 End of yr. 2
$2.31 + 1.00 End of yr. 3 = $3.31 × 10% = .33	$3.31 + .33 = $3.64 End of yr. 3
$3.64 + 1.00 End of yr. 4 = $4.64 × 10% = . 46	$4.64 + .46 = $5.10 End of yr. 4
$5.10 + 1.00 End of yr. 5 = $6.10 × 10% = .61	$6.10 + .61 = $6.71 End of yr. 5
$6.71 + 1.00 End of yr. 6 = $7.71 × 10% = .77	$7.71 + .77 = 8.48 End of yr. 6
$8.48 + 1.00 End of yr. 7 = $9.48 × 10% = . 95	$9.48 + .95 = 10.43 End of yr. 7
$10.43 + 1.00 End of yr. 8 = $11.43 × 10% = 1.14	$11.43 + 1.14 = $12.57 End of yr. 8
$12.57 + 1.00 End of yr. 9 = $13.57 × 10% = $1.36	$13.57 + 1.36 = $14.93 End of yr. 9
$14.93 + 1.00 End of yr. 10 = $15.93	

Method 2. Multiply the initial investment by 100 percent plus the interest rate. Add the additional investment. Repeat for each of the ten years.

$ 1.00	End of yr. 1		$ 6.71	End of yr. 6
× 110%			+ 1.00	End of yr. 6
$ 1.10			$ 7.71	Beginning of yr. 7
+ 1.00	End of yr. 2		× 110%	
$ 2.10	End of yr. 2		$ 8.48	End of yr. 7
× 110%			+ 1.00	End of yr. 7
$ 2.31	End of yr. 3		$ 9.48	Beginning of yr. 8
+ 1.00	End of yr. 3		× 110%	
$ 3.31	Beginning of yr. 4		$10.43	End of yr. 8
× 110%			+ 1.00	End of yr. 8
$ 3.64	End of yr. 4		$11.43	Beginning of yr. 9
+ 1.00	End of yr. 4		× 110%	
$ 4.64	Beginning of yr. 5		$12.57	End of yr. 9
× 110%			+ 1.00	End of yr. 9
$ 5.10	End of yr. 5		$13.57	Beginning of yr. 10
+ 1.00	End of yr. 5		× 110%	
$ 6.10	Beginning of yr. 6		$14.93	End of yr. 10
× 110%			+ 1.00	End of yr. 10
$ 6.71	End of yr. 6		$15.93	

Method 3. Use the compound interest table and find the appropriate factor for the interest rate and term. Multiply the initial investment by the factor.

Now use Table B to look up the factor for 10 percent return for ten years. Note that the factor is 15.937 (rounded). Multiply the lump sum of $1 by 15.937 = $15.94 (rounded). Again, using the table is much simpler! In other words, the annuity table reveals the future value of $1.

Problem B.   Now, using Table B, calculate the future value of $2,000 at 10 percent in ten years if $2,000 is added every year.

$2,000 × 15.937 = $31,874 (rounded)

Problem C.   Also using Table B, calculate the future value of $2,000 at 10 percent for 20 years if $2,000 is added every year.

$2,000 × 57.275 = $114,550

These calculations demonstrate the use of Table B to determine the *future value* of present income when the income stream is an annuity.

■ Present Value of Future Income Computed Using Table B

We can also use Table B to consider the *present value* of future income. Using the last problem, consider a 45-year-old investor's desire to have $1,000,000 saved up by the time he is 75 years old. Assume that the investor can experience an average 7 percent yield during the 30 years it takes for him to reach his retirement age. By using Table B, we can calculate that the investor will have to save approximately $10,586 every year in order to meet that goal.

$$\frac{\$1,000,000 \div 94.461}{\text{future value}} = \frac{\$10,586}{\text{present value}}$$

Another realistic problem that can be solved using Table B is saving for a child's education.

Problem. Say that the projected cost of a good four-year university will be $75,000 (room, board, tuition). If parents have 18 years before their child goes to college and can budget the same amount every year for an investment with a guaranteed 5 percent yield, how much do they have to save every year to achieve their goal?

$$\frac{\$75,000 \div 28.132}{\text{future value}} = \frac{\$2,666}{\text{present value}}$$

■ Calculating After-Tax Sales Proceeds

To determine the financial management rate of return (FMRR), investors and real estate professionals have to project the after-tax sales proceeds of an investment years into the future as well as determine that investment's present value.

The calculation of after-tax cash flow was discussed in the previous chapter. Tables A and B will be used in the FMRR calculation to determine what the projected after-tax cash flow from a real estate investment will be in the future. There are five steps involved.

Step 1. Calculate the projected value or sales price

The first step in determining the after-tax sales proceeds is to guess at the annual appreciation rate (based on research of past trends) and/or to ask the investor what appreciation rate should be used. (To avoid serious miscalculation and disappointment, real estate professionals should always use conservative figures rather than unrealistic ones.) Investors must also provide the expected holding period of the investment. Again, it is better to use shorter rather than longer terms in the calculation because it is difficult to project what will happen to other variables over a long forecast. Factors such as appreciation and tax laws and their consequences can change very quickly. A five-year or ten-year projected holding period may be appropriate.

Problem. Remember the Otts' investment in a condominium first discussed in Chapter 5? Let's assume that the Otts plan to sell the condominium after owning it for five years. Let's also assume that it is likely that properties will appreciate 5 percent annually, based on economic forecasts and regional factors. Using

Table A, estimate the value or projected sales price of the condominium five years from now.

Solution.

Purchase price	$100,000	
Table A factor	× 1.276	(5 years, 5%)
Value/sales price	$127,600	

Step 2. Project the cost of sale and determine the realized sales price

The next step is to project the cost of selling the condominium five years from now. The cost of sale is typically provided by the investor or by the real estate professional. Generally, the cost of the sale will include the sales commission or fee that will be charged by the real estate professional and/or any marketing costs. The projected costs of sale are deducted from the projected sales price to determine the *realized sales price*.

Problem.   Let's assume that the Otts estimate that the projected cost of sale will be 6 percent on the projected value or sales price of $127,600. Calculate the projected cost of sale on the Otts' condominium.

Solution.

Projected sales price	$127,600
– Projected sales cost (6%)	– 7,656
Projected realized sales price	$119,944

Step 3. Calculate capital gain on the sale

The next step in calculating after-tax proceeds is to determine the capital gain. Capital gains on an investment are handled differently from capital gains on investment property. To determine gain on a sale of investment property, investors must also know the *acquisition cost*, that is, how much they paid for the property plus closing costs. The difference between the realized sales price and the total acquisition cost is the amount of capital gain that will be reported to the IRS.

Problem.   Recall that the Otts paid $100,000 for the condominium as well as another $3,000 for closing costs. In Step 2 above, we determined the projected value or sales price of the condominium five years from now is $119,944. What is the capital gain the Otts will experience five years from now when they sell their condominium?

Solution.

Projected realized sales price	$119,944
– Total acquisition (purchase price + closing costs)	– 103,000
Capital gain	$ 16,944

The amount of tax that may be due depends on several factors: (1) The taxpayer's tax bracket, which determines the capital gains tax. For tax year 2004, high-bracketed taxpayers pay 15 percent capital gains tax; lower-bracketed taxpayers pay 5 percent. (2) How much of the purchase price, if any, is received in cash. If cash is received, capital gains tax is due on the reporting of the sale. (3) If the sale were an exchange, tax owed could be deferred indefinitely.

(Note: For purposes of calculating the FMRR, the assumption is that the investor will sell the investment property for cash at the end of the holding period. However, it is advisable for investors to seek the counsel of their tax and legal advisers about the possibilities of getting involved in a tax-deferred exchange. Real estate practitioners would be well-advised to take courses or read texts on tax-deferred exchanges, which can be a very beneficial method of selling investment property—for investors and their agents alike.)

Step 4. Calculate the capital gains tax due

Assume that this investment will be owned by an affluent taxpayer in the 33 percent tax bracket. Thus, the tax owed on the capital gain would be calculated as follows:

Capital gain	$16,944
× Appropriate capital gains tax	× 15%
Capital gains tax owed	$ 2,542

Unfortunately, more tax is owed on the sale because the investor took depreciation deductions during the holding period. At the time of sale, the depreciation is recaptured and taxed at a 25 percent rate.

Problem A.   Recall that the Otts' annual depreciation deduction will be $3,371. They will take this deduction for each of the five years they own the property. At the time of sale, the depreciation will be recaptured at a 25 percent rate. Calculate the depreciation recapture.

Solution.

Depreciation yearly	$ 3,371
× Holding period	× 5
Depreciation recapture	$16,855
× Depreciation recapture tax	× 25%
Depreciation recapture tax due	$ 4,214

Problem B.   What is the total tax due on the sale of the Otts' investment if they must pay the capital gains tax of $2,542 and depreciation recapture tax of $4,214?

Solution.

Capital gains tax	$2,542
+ Depreciation recapture tax	+4,214
Total tax due	$6,756

Step 5. Calculate the net after-tax sales proceeds

The last step in determining the net after-tax proceeds is to subtract all the expenses of the sale from the projected sales price. The expenses include the costs of sale and taxes discussed earlier.

In addition, the mortgage balance must also be deducted from the projected sales price because we assume that the investors will pay off their loan. For simplicity's sake, we will assume that there has been no reduction of mortgage balance and use the original amount of the loan. (For the typical investment held less than ten years, the rate of return using an interest-only loan turns out be less than ½ of 1 percent different from that calculated for a conventional type loan due to the small principal reduction in the first years of a loan. However, it should be noted that the impact of mortgage reduction over the long term on the FMRR can be significant.)

Thus, the formula for calculating *net after-tax sales proceeds* is

$$\text{Net After-Tax Sales Proceeds} =$$
$$\text{Projected Sales Price} - (\text{Sales Costs} + \text{Mortgage Balance} + \text{Tax Due})$$

Problem. Let's review the Otts' investment. The projected sales price of the condominium is $127,600. The costs of sale are $7,656. The taxes due are $6,756. The original mortgage balance is $85,000. After all the expenses of the sale are paid, what is the Otts' after-tax sales proceeds?

Solution.

Projected sales price	$127,600
Less costs of sale	− 7,656
Less mortgage balance	− 85,000
Less tax due	− 6,756
Net after-tax sales proceeds	$ 28,188

The calculation of the net after-tax sales proceeds is a future lump sum that will be a necessary part of determining the FMRR.

■ Summary

The promise of an investment's future income from periodic income and sales proceeds has value today. Using compound interest tables is the easiest method of calculating the present value of future income, information that is necessary to determine the FMRR.

There are five steps in calculating net after-tax sales proceeds. First, calculate the projected value or sales price. Second, project the costs of sale and determine the realized sales price, then subtract them from the projected sales price to obtain the realized sales price. Third, calculate the capital gain on the sale. Fourth, calculate the capital gains tax due. The last step in determining the net after-tax proceeds is to subtract all the expenses of the sale, including loan payoff, from the projected sales price.

Table A. Future Value of $1 Lump Sum (or the Value of $1 Saved Each Year) Compounded at Various Interest Rates for Various Periods

Year	1%	2%	3%	4%	5%	6%	7%	8%	9%	10%
1	1.010	1.020	1.030	1.040	1.050	1.060	1.070	1.080	1.090	1.100
2	1.020	1.040	1.061	1.082	1.103	1.124	1.145	1.166	1.188	1.210
3	1.030	1.061	1.093	1.125	1.158	1.191	1.225	1.260	1.295	1.331
4	1.041	1.082	1.126	1.170	1.216	1.262	1.311	1.360	1.412	1.464
5	1.051	1.104	1.159	1.217	1.276	1.338	1.403	1.469	1.539	1.611
6	1.062	1.126	1.194	1.265	1.340	1.419	1.501	1.587	1.677	1.772
7	1.072	1.149	1.230	1.316	1.407	1.504	1.606	1.714	1.828	1.949
8	1.083	1.172	1.267	1.369	1.477	1.594	1.718	1.851	1.993	2.144
9	1.094	1.195	1.305	1.423	1.551	1.689	1.838	1.999	2.172	2.358
10	1.105	1.219	1.344	1.480	1.629	1.791	1.967	2.159	2.367	2.594
11	1.116	1.243	1.384	1.539	1.710	1.898	2.105	2.332	2.580	2.853
12	1.127	1.268	1.426	1.601	1.796	2.012	2.252	2.518	2.813	3.138
13	1.138	1.294	1.469	1.665	1.886	2.133	2.410	2.720	3.066	3.452
14	1.149	1.319	1.513	1.732	1.980	2.261	2.579	2.937	3.342	3.797
15	1.161	1.346	1.558	1.801	2.079	2.397	2.759	3.172	3.642	4.177
16	1.173	1.373	1.605	1.873	2.183	2.540	2.952	3.426	3.970	4.595
17	1.184	1.400	1.653	1.948	2.292	2.693	3.159	3.700	4.328	5.054
18	1.196	1.428	1.702	2.026	2.407	2.854	3.380	3.996	4.717	5.560
19	1.208	1.457	1.754	2.107	2.527	3.026	3.617	4.316	5.142	6.116
20	1.220	1.486	1.806	2.191	2.653	3.207	3.870	4.661	5.604	6.727
21	1.232	1.516	1.860	2.279	2.786	3.400	4.141	5.034	6.109	7.400
22	1.245	1.546	1.916	2.370	2.925	3.604	4.430	5.437	6.659	8.140
23	1.257	1.577	1.974	2.465	3.072	3.820	4.741	5.871	7.258	8.954
24	1.270	1.608	2.033	2.563	3.225	4.049	5.072	6.341	7.911	9.850
25	1.282	1.641	2.094	2.666	3.386	4.292	5.427	6.848	8.623	10.835
26	1.295	1.673	2.157	2.772	3.556	4.549	5.807	7.396	9.399	11.918
27	1.308	1.707	2.221	2.883	3.733	4.822	6.214	7.988	10.245	13.110
28	1.321	1.741	2.288	2.999	3.920	5.112	6.649	8.627	11.167	14.421
29	1.335	1.776	2.357	3.119	4.116	5.418	7.114	9.317	12.172	15.863
30	1.348	1.811	2.427	3.243	4.322	5.743	7.612	10.063	13.268	17.449

Year	11%	12%	13%	14%	15%	16%	17%	18%	19%	20%
1	1.110	1.120	1.130	1.140	1.150	1.160	1.170	1.180	1.190	01.20
2	1.232	1.254	1.277	1.300	1.323	1.346	1.369	1.392	1.416	01.44
3	1.368	1.405	1.443	1.482	1.521	1.561	1.602	1.643	1.685	01.73
4	1.518	1.574	1.630	1.689	1.749	1.811	1.874	1.939	2.005	02.07
5	1.685	1.762	1.842	1.925	2.011	2.100	2.192	2.288	2.386	02.49
6	1.870	1.974	2.082	2.195	2.313	2.436	2.565	2.700	2.840	02.99
7	2.076	2.211	2.353	2.502	2.660	2.826	3.001	3.185	3.379	03.58
8	2.305	2.476	2.658	2.853	3.059	3.278	3.511	3.759	4.021	04.30
9	2.558	2.773	3.004	3.252	3.518	3.803	4.108	4.435	4.785	05.16
10	2.839	3.106	3.395	3.707	4.046	4.411	4.807	5.234	5.695	06.19
11	3.152	3.479	3.836	4.226	4.652	5.117	5.624	6.176	6.777	07.43
12	3.498	3.896	4.335	4.818	5.350	5.936	6.580	7.288	8.064	08.92
13	3.883	4.363	4.898	5.492	6.153	6.886	7.699	8.599	9.596	10.70
14	4.310	4.887	5.535	6.261	7.076	7.988	9.007	10.147	11.420	12.84
15	4.785	5.474	6.254	7.138	8.137	9.266	10.539	11.974	13.590	15.41
16	5.311	6.130	7.067	8.137	9.358	10.748	12.330	14.129	16.172	18.49
17	5.895	6.866	7.986	9.276	10.761	12.468	14.426	16.672	19.244	22.19
18	6.544	7.690	9.024	10.575	12.375	14.463	16.879	19.673	22.901	26.62
19	7.263	8.613	10.197	12.056	14.232	16.777	19.748	23.214	27.252	31.95
20	8.062	9.646	11.523	13.743	16.367	19.461	23.106	27.393	32.429	38.34
21	8.949	10.804	13.021	15.668	18.822	22.574	27.034	32.324	38.591	46.01
22	9.934	12.100	14.714	17.861	21.645	26.186	31.629	38.142	45.923	55.21
23	11.026	13.552	16.627	20.362	24.891	30.376	37.006	45.008	54.649	66.25
24	12.239	15.179	18.788	23.212	28.625	35.236	43.297	53.109	65.032	79.50
25	13.585	17.000	21.231	26.462	32.919	40.874	50.658	62.669	77.388	95.40
26	15.080	19.040	23.991	30.167	37.857	47.414	59.270	73.949	92.092	114.48
27	16.739	21.325	27.109	34.390	43.535	55.000	69.345	87.260	109.589	137.37
28	18.580	23.884	30.633	39.204	50.066	63.800	81.134	102.967	130.411	164.84
29	20.624	26.750	34.616	44.693	57.575	74.009	94.927	121.501	155.189	197.81
30	22.892	29.960	39.116	50.950	66.212	85.850	111.065	143.371	184.675	237.38

Table B. Future Value of $1 Annuity (or the Value of $1 Saved Each Year + $1 Added Each Year) Compounded at Various Interest Rates for Various Periods

Year	1%	2%	3%	4%	5%	6%	7%	8%	9%	10%
1	1.000	1.000	1.000	1.000	1.000	1.000	1.000	1.000	1.000	1.000
2	2.010	2.020	2.030	2.040	2.050	2.060	2.070	2.080	2.090	2.100
3	3.030	3.060	3.091	3.122	3.153	3.184	3.215	3.246	3.278	3.310
4	4.060	4.122	4.184	4.246	4.310	4.375	4.440	4.506	4.573	4.640
5	5.101	5.204	5.309	5.416	5.526	5.637	5.751	5.867	5.985	6.100
6	6.152	6.308	6.468	6.633	6.802	6.975	7.153	7.336	7.523	7.710
7	7.214	7.434	7.662	7.898	8.142	8.394	8.654	8.923	9.200	9.480
8	8.286	8.583	8.892	9.214	9.549	9.897	10.260	10.637	11.028	11.430
9	9.369	9.755	10.159	10.583	11.027	11.491	11.978	12.488	13.021	13.570
10	10.462	10.950	11.464	12.006	12.578	13.181	13.816	14.487	15.193	15.930
11	11.567	12.169	12.808	13.486	14.207	14.972	15.784	16.645	17.560	18.530
12	12.683	13.412	14.192	15.026	15.917	16.870	17.888	18.977	20.141	21.380
13	13.809	14.680	15.618	16.627	17.713	18.882	20.141	21.495	22.953	24.520
14	14.947	15.974	17.086	18.292	19.599	21.015	22.550	24.215	26.019	27.970
15	16.097	17.293	18.599	20.024	21.579	23.276	25.129	27.152	29.361	31.770
16	17.258	18.639	20.157	21.825	23.657	25.673	27.888	30.324	33.003	35.950
17	18.430	20.012	21.762	23.698	25.840	28.213	30.840	33.750	36.974	40.540
18	19.615	21.412	23.414	25.645	28.132	30.906	33.999	37.450	41.301	45.590
19	20.811	22.841	25.117	27.671	30.539	33.760	37.379	41.446	46.018	51.150
20	22.019	24.297	26.870	29.778	33.066	36.786	40.995	45.762	51.160	57.270
21	23.239	25.783	28.676	31.969	35.719	39.993	44.865	50.423	56.765	64.000
22	24.472	27.299	30.537	34.248	38.505	43.392	49.006	55.457	62.873	71.400
23	25.716	28.845	32.453	36.618	41.430	46.996	53.436	60.893	69.532	79.540
24	26.973	30.422	34.426	39.083	44.502	50.816	58.177	66.765	76.790	88.490
25	28.243	32.030	36.459	41.646	47.727	54.865	63.249	73.106	84.701	98.340
26	29.526	33.671	38.553	44.312	51.113	59.156	68.676	79.954	93.324	109.18
27	30.821	35.344	40.710	47.084	54.669	63.706	74.484	87.351	102.723	121.10
28	32.129	37.051	42.931	49.968	58.403	68.528	80.698	95.339	112.968	134.21
29	33.450	38.792	45.219	52.966	62.323	73.640	87.347	103.966	124.135	148.63
30	34.785	40.568	47.575	56.085	66.439	79.058	94.461	113.283	136.308	164.49

Year	11%	12%	13%	14%	15%	16%	17%	18%	19%	20%
1	1.000	1.000	1.000	1.000	1.000	1.000	1.000	1.000	1.000	1.000
2	2.110	2.120	2.130	2.140	2.150	2.160	2.170	2.180	2.190	2.200
3	3.342	3.374	3.407	3.440	3.473	3.506	3.539	3.572	3.606	3.640
4	4.710	4.779	4.850	4.921	4.993	5.066	5.141	5.215	5.291	5.368
5	6.228	6.353	6.480	6.610	6.742	6.877	7.014	7.154	7.297	7.442
6	7.913	8.115	8.323	8.536	8.754	8.977	9.207	9.442	9.683	9.930
7	9.783	10.089	10.405	10.730	11.067	11.414	11.772	12.142	12.523	12.916
8	11.859	12.300	12.757	13.233	13.727	14.240	14.773	15.327	15.902	16.499
9	14.164	14.776	15.416	16.085	16.786	17.519	18.285	19.086	19.923	20.799
10	16.722	17.549	18.420	19.337	20.304	21.321	22.393	23.521	24.709	25.959
11	19.561	20.655	21.814	23.045	24.349	25.733	27.200	28.755	30.404	32.150
12	22.713	24.133	25.650	27.271	29.002	30.850	32.824	34.931	37.180	39.581
13	26.212	28.029	29.985	32.089	34.352	36.786	39.404	42.219	45.244	48.497
14	30.095	32.393	34.883	37.581	40.505	43.672	47.103	50.818	54.841	59.196
15	34.405	37.280	40.417	43.842	47.580	51.660	56.110	60.965	66.261	72.035
16	39.190	42.753	46.672	50.980	55.717	60.925	66.649	72.939	79.850	87.442
17	44.501	48.884	53.739	59.118	65.075	71.673	78.979	87.068	96.022	105.931
18	50.396	55.750	61.725	68.394	75.836	84.141	93.406	103.740	115.266	128.117
19	56.939	63.440	70.749	78.969	88.212	98.603	110.285	123.414	138.166	154.740
20	64.203	72.052	80.947	91.025	102.444	115.380	130.033	146.628	165.418	186.688
21	72.265	81.699	92.470	104.768	118.810	134.841	153.139	174.021	197.847	225.026
22	81.214	92.503	105.491	120.436	137.632	157.415	180.172	206.345	236.438	271.031
23	91.148	104.603	120.205	138.297	159.276	183.601	211.801	244.487	282.362	326.237
24	102.174	118.155	136.831	158.659	184.168	213.978	248.808	289.494	337.010	392.484
25	114.413	133.334	155.620	181.871	212.793	249.214	292.105	342.603	402.042	471.981
26	127.999	150.334	176.850	208.333	245.712	290.088	342.763	405.272	479.431	567.377
27	143.079	169.374	200.841	238.499	283.569	337.502	402.032	479.221	571.522	681.853
28	159.817	190.699	227.950	272.889	327.104	392.503	471.378	566.481	681.112	819.223
29	178.397	214.583	258.583	312.094	377.170	456.303	552.512	669.447	811.523	984.068
30	199.021	241.333	293.199	356.787	434.745	530.312	647.439	790.948	966.712	1181.882

■ Chapter 7 Review Questions

1. To calculate the present value of future income, investors should use
   a. the compound interest tables.
   b. the kitchen table.
   c. the FMRR.
   d. capitalization rates.

2. An example of lump sum income from a real estate investment is
   a. before-tax yearly rental income.
   b. net operating income.
   c. after-tax proceeds of the sale.
   d. cash throw-off.

3. An example of an annuity income from a real estate investment is
   a. annual after-tax income.
   b. after-tax proceeds of the sale.
   c. depreciation deductions.
   d. potential gross income.

4. Table A is used to calculate
   a. future value of $1 invested today.
   b. future value of $1 invested today plus another $1 invested annually.
   c. present value of $1 invested tomorrow.
   d. present value of $1 invested tomorrow less $1 withdrawn annually.

5. Table B is used to calculate
   a. future value of $1 invested today.
   b. future value of $1 invested today plus another $1 invested annually.
   c. present value of $1 invested tomorrow.
   d. present value of $1 invested tomorrow less $1 withdrawn annually.

6. An investor purchased a $98,000 commercial building that will be held for ten years. Assuming tax laws do not change during that period, what tax will be owed on the depreciation recapture if the building is sold for cash at the end of the holding period?
   a. $6,282
   b. $8,909
   c. $9,800
   d. Cannot be determined

7. Investors wish to invest $550,000 in an office building, anticipating an 8 percent yield. They plan to cash out within five years. The appropriate factor for five years at 8 percent is 1.469. What is the future value of their investment if their assumptions are correct?
   a. $374,404
   b. $807,950
   c. $1,908,000
   d. $2,800,000

8. An investor wishes to have his savings total $1,000,000 before his 65th birthday. He is now 35 years old. He can invest in a bond with a guaranteed 3 percent yield. How much will he have to pay for this bond today if the factor is 2.427?
   a. $223,000
   b. $304,950
   c. $400,031
   d. $412,031

9. An investor believes that her real estate investment will provide an after-tax income of $2,500 annually for ten years. If her investment provides a 5 percent yield, what is the present value of that annuity income (factor = 12.578)?
   a. $11,250
   b. $18,600
   c. $22,500
   d. $31,445

10. Investors project that the sales price of their investment will be $1,000,000 and that sales costs will run around 7.5 percent. Their mortgage balance will be approximately $250,000 and taxes due on the sale will be $16,000. What are the estimated after-tax sales proceeds?
    a. $659,000
    b. $687,500
    c. $887,400
    d. $895,200

Using the Financial Management Rate of Return

chapter eight

learning objectives

After completing this chapter, you will be able to

■ calculate the after-tax investment rate;

■ calculate total future wealth;

■ calculate financial management rate of return; and

■ appropriately apply the terms *after-tax investment rate* and *total future wealth.*

■ Key Terms

after-tax investment rate   total future wealth

■ Introduction

Without the use of financial calculators or spreadsheets, calculating the financial management rate of return (FMRR) can be a rather tedious and complex matter. However, for investment novices, calculating the FMRR with the use of the following worksheets can be a meaningful exercise. Even investment experts can benefit from using these worksheets and then later make the transition to spreadsheets.

Five worksheets are contained in this section to assist in calculating the FMRR. Note that all significant entries are keyed by letters of the alphabet to assist students in making the appropriate entries.

Calculating the FMRR for a Residential Condominium

Let's review the Otts' purchase of a residential condominium: The property address is 111 Condo Drive. The closing is taking place today. Mr. and Mrs. Ott are paying $100,000, putting $15,000 down, and taking out a first mortgage of $85,000 at 8.5 percent for 30 years. The interest on the loan is approximately $7,225 yearly; the amount paid toward principal is $600 yearly. There is no other financing on this property. Closing costs are $3,000.

The Otts' tax adviser suggests it would be appropriate to attribute 90 percent of the purchase price and closing costs to the building and only 10 percent to the land. The Otts' real estate broker has given them a pro forma with the following projections:

Monthly rent (potential)	$1,100
Vacancy allowance	5%
Property taxes	$1,700
Insurance	$200
Utilities	paid by tenants
Maintenance	$1,800 yearly

The Otts are in the 28 percent tax bracket. They plan to hold on to this investment for five years and expect that it will appreciate by 5 percent each year. When they sell it, they can expect that costs will run about 6 percent of the sales price.

If the Otts did not purchase this condominium as an investment, they would be likely to find an alternative investment yielding a before-tax investment rate of 3 percent.

Before-Tax and After-Tax Investment Rate

The Otts have indicated that they believe they can earn 3 percent on their investments (investor's before-tax or pre-tax rate). They may be considering bonds, for example, as an alternative to an investment in this condominium. The 3 percent *pre-tax* rate must be converted to an *after-tax* rate so that a comparison can be made between the investor's stipulated yield of 3 percent and the FMRR on the real estate investment. FMRR is an after-tax rate of return.

To make the conversion, we must calculate what the IRS will leave the investor after taxes. If the investor is in the 28 percent tax bracket, then the investor will have 72 percent of his anticipated yield, or

$$100\% - 28\% = 72\%$$

If the investor's desired rate of return is 3 percent before taxes, then the investor will have 72 percent of the 3 percent left after taxes, or

$$3\% \times 72\% = 2.16\% \text{ after-tax rate}$$

The 2.16 percent reflects the real after-tax rate that the investor may receive on bonds or other alternative investments. The 2.16 percent rate also indicates the benchmark for the real estate investment being considered. The real estate investment's estimated FMRR must be competitive with 2.16 percent or why would the investor choose the real estate investment over the alternative?

■ Worksheet 1: Property Summary

Problem

Apply the information from the case study to Worksheet 1 on the next page. Complete the necessary calculations.

1100
&
2200
00
3200

13,200
.05
660.00

Worksheet 1: Property Summary

Property address: _____ m Condo Drive _____

Investor: _____ Otis _____ Date: _____ 6/1/00 _____

Purchase price: _____ 100,000 _____ [a]

Add closing costs: _____ 3600 _____ [b]

Total acquisition cost: _____ 103 000 _____ [c]

Improvement allocation: × _____ %

Improvement value: _____ [d]

1st mortgage: _____ 85,000 _____ [e] × rate _____ 8.5 _____ % =   Interest _____ [f]

Principal: _____ [g]

Debt service: _____ [h]

Down payment: $ _____ 15,000 _____

Add closing costs: + _____ 3,000 _____ [b]

Initial investment $ _____ 18,000 _____ [i]

Gross monthly income: $ _____ 1,100 _____ × 12 = yrly. gross income: $ _____ 13,200 _____ [j]

Annual vacancy allowance: _____ 5 _____ % × yrly. gross income [j] = $ _____ 660 _____ [k]

Annual Operating Expenses

Property taxes: $ _____

Insurance: + $ _____

Utilities: + $ _____

Maintenance: + $ _____

Other: + $ _____

Annual operating expenses: $ _____ [l]

Investor's tax bracket _____ % [m]

Holding period: _____ yrs. [n]

Ann. appreciation: _____ % [o]

Proj. cost of sale: _____ % [p]

Inv. pre-tax rate: _____ %

100% – _____ % tax bracket [m] = × _____ %

After-tax rate: _____ % [q] (rounded) (*This rate is the investor's desired after-tax rate of return. This rate should be contrasted with the FMRR on Worksheet 5.*)

■ Worksheet 2: Before-Tax Cash Flow

The completion of Worksheet 2 will help investors determine the before-tax cash flow on the property.

Problem

Take the information from the Otts' purchase described earlier and from Worksheet 1 and enter it on Worksheet 2. Complete the necessary calculations.

Worksheet 2: Before-Tax Cash Flow

Potential gross income: _____ [j]

Less vacancy allowance: − _____ [k]

Effective gross operating income: _____

Less total operating expenses: − _____ [l]

Net operating income: _____ [r]

Less debt service payments: − _____ [h]

Before-tax cash flow (BTCF): _____ [s]

■ Worksheet 3: After-Tax Cash Flow

The completion of Worksheet 3 will help investors determine the after-tax cash flow on the property.

Problem

Take the information from the Otts' purchase as described and from Worksheets 1 and 2 and enter it on Worksheet 3. Complete the necessary calculations.

Worksheet 3: After-Tax Cash Flow

Net operating income:	$_____ [r]	
Less annual interest payment:	− $_____ [f]	
Less depreciation:	− $_____ [t]	
Taxable income/loss:	$_____	
× Tax bracket:	×_____ [m]	
Tax savings (if *negative*) or tax liability (if *positive*):	$_____ [u]	

Depreciation Calculation

Improvement
value $_____[d]

Divided by   (hint:
economic life   ÷_____ condo)
       27.5 or 39 years

Annual depreciation
deduction $_____[t]

Before-tax cash flow:	$_____ [s]
Add tax savings or subtract tax liability:	+$_____ [u]
After-tax cash flow:	$_____ [v]

■ Worksheet 4: After-Tax Proceeds from the Sale

The completion of Worksheet 4 will help investors determine the after-tax sales proceeds on the property. (Recall that we indicated earlier that for the sake of simplicity, no principal reduction on the mortgage was included in the calculation of the FMRR.)

Problem

Take the information from the Otts' purchase and from Worksheets 1, 2, and 3 and enter it on Worksheet 4. Complete the necessary calculations.

Worksheet 4: After-Tax Proceeds from the Sale

Purchase price: $_____[a]

Annual appreciation rate: _____%[o]

Holding period: _____ yrs.[n] [Use Table A] (Hint: factor = 1.276)

Projected sales price: $_____ [w]

Less cost of sale: _____% − $_____ [p]

Realized sales price: $_____

Less total acquisition: − $_____ [c]

Capital gain: $_____

× Max. cap. gain tax (15% or 5%): × _____%

Capital gain tax due: $_____

Add deprec. recap. tax: + $_____ ◄

Tax due from sale: $_____[x]

Depreciation Recapture

_____yrs._____holding period [n]
× $_____depreciation [t]
= $_____total depreciation
× __25%__ deprec. recap. tax rate
$_____deprec. recap. tax

Note: If sellers receive cash from the sale of their investment, the tax cannot be postponed. Sellers should consider a 1031-tax-deferred exchange before selling for cash.

Projected sales price: $_____[w]

Less sales costs: − $_____[p]

Less mtg. balance: − $_____[e]

Less tax due: − $_____[x]

Net after-tax proceeds: $_____[y]

■ Worksheet 5: Performance Summary with FMRR

And now for the dramatic finish! The completion of Worksheet 5 will help investors summarize the impact of all the investment property's cash flow as well as determine the FMRR.

Part 1

There are two parts to completing Worksheet 5: first, we must calculate the *total future wealth* that this investment provides: not only the net after-tax proceeds calculated in Worksheet 4 ($28,188) but also the value of the after-tax cash flow calculated in Worksheet 3 ($1,507) that the property has provided each year of the holding period (5 years).

Problem

Using Table B, calculate the future value of the after-tax cash flow. (**Hint:** Table B does not provide factors for 2.16 percent, so use 2 percent. The factor is 5.204.) Now complete the first part of Worksheet 5 based on the Otts' purchase and previous worksheets.

Worksheet 5, Part 1: Performance Summary with FMRR

After-tax cash flow: $_____ [v]

Investor after-tax rate of return: _____ % [q]

Holding period: _____ yrs. [n] [Use Table B]

Amount accumulated: $_____

Plus net after-tax proceeds from sale: + $_____ [y]

Total future wealth: $_____

Part 2

To complete Worksheet 5 in its entirety and calculate the property's FMRR, investors must ask, "What rate of return did I receive if I invested $18,000 in this condominium for five years and received $36,030 at the end of the holding period?" While a financial spreadsheet or calculator could do this calculation in seconds, calculating the FMRR is more tedious. The investor must actually play a guessing game and use Table B to answer this question.

Problem

For example, let's guess that the Otts received 10 percent on their investment. Using Table A, we find that the factor for 10 percent for five years is 1.611.

> $18,000   Present Value
> × 1.611
> $28,998   Future Value

The $28,998 is too low because the investor can anticipate $36,030, so our guess at the FMRR must have been too low. Could the rate have been 12 percent? At 12 percent, the factor is 1.762.

> $18,000   Present Value
> × 1.762
> $31,716   Future Value

The $31,716 is still too low. Could the rate have been 14 percent? At 14 percent, the factor is 1.925.

> $18,000   Present Value
> × 1.925
> $34,650   Future Value

We're getting warmer! However, we are trying to find the correct rate so that the future value is as close to $36,030 as possible. Could the rate be 15 percent? At 15 percent, the factor is 2.011.

> $18,000   Present Value
> × 2.01
> $36,180   Future Value

In this case, the 15 percent rate indicates that we have exceeded $36,030, the anticipated total future wealth this building will generate. So we can assume that the FMRR is somewhere just under 15 percent. In fact, with a spread sheet or financial calculator, we would have been able to determine that the actual FMRR is

> Financial Management Rate of Return (Yield) [I]   14.92 %

Problem

Take the information for Case Study 1 and from Worksheets 1, 2, 3, and 4 and enter it on Worksheet 5.

Worksheet 5, Parts 1 and 2: Performance Summary with FMRR

After-tax cash flow:	$_____ [v]
Investor after-tax rate of return:	_____%[q]
Holding period:	_____ yrs.[n] [Use Table B]
Amount accumulated:	$_____
Plus net after-tax proceeds from sale:	+$_____ [y]
Total future wealth:	$_____
Initial investment:	$_____ [i]
Holding period:	_____ yrs.[n]
Financial Management Rate of Return (Yield):	_____% [Use Table A]

Completed Worksheets 1 through 5 follow.

Completed Worksheet 1: Property Summary

Property address: _____111 Condo Drive_____

Investor: _____Otts_____   Date: _____Today_____

Purchase price: _____100,000_____ [a]

Add closing costs: _____3,000_____ [b]

Total acquisition cost: _____103,000_____ [c]

Improvement allocation   × _____90_____ %

Improvement value _____92,700_____ [d]

1st mortgage:_____85,000_____ [e] × rate __8.5__ % =   Interest _____7,225_____ [f]

Principal: + _____600_____ [g]

Debt service   _____7,825_____ [h]

Down payment: $_____15,000_____

Add closing costs   + _____3,000_____ [b]

Initial investment: $_____18,000_____ [i]

Gross monthly income: $___1,100_____ × 12 = yrly. gross income: $___13,200_____ [j]

Annual vacancy allowance: ____5____ % × yrly. gross income [j] = $_____660_____ [k]

Annual Operating Expenses

Property taxes: $__1,700_____

Insurance: + $__200_____

Utilities: + $__pd. by tenant__

Maintenance: + $__1,800_____

Other: + $__0_____

Annual operating expenses: $__3,700___ [l]

Investor's tax bracket ___28____ % [m]

Holding period: ____5____ yrs. [n]

Ann. appreciation: ____5____ % [o]

Proj. cost of sale: ____6____ % [p]

Inv. pre-tax rate: ___3_ %

(100% − _____% tax bracket [m] = × ___72__ %

After-tax rate: ___2__ % [q] (rounded) *(This rate is the investor's desired after-tax rate of return. This rate should be contrasted with the FMRR on Worksheet 5.)*

Completed Worksheet 2: Before-Tax Cash Flow

Potential gross income:		13,200	[j]
Less vacancy allowance	–	660	[k]
Effective gross operating income:		12,540	
Less total operating expenses	–	3,700	[l]
Net operating income:		8,840	[r]
Less debt service payments	–	7,825	[h]
Before-tax cash flow (BTCF)		1,015	[s]

Completed Worksheet 3: After-Tax Cash Flow

Net operating income	$ 8,840	[r]	
Less annual interest payment	– $ 7,225	[f]	
Less depreciation	– $ 3,371	[t]	
Taxable income/loss	– $ 1,756		
× tax bracket	× $ 28%	[m]	
Tax savings (if *negative*) or tax liability (if *positive*)	– $ 492	[u]	

Depreciation Calculation

Improvement value	$ 92,700	[d]
Divided by economic life	+ 27.5 (condo) 27.5 or 39 years	
Annual depreciation deduction	$ 3,371	[t]

Before-tax cash flow:	$ 1,015	[s]
Add tax savings or subtract tax liability:	+ $ 492	[u]
After-tax cash flow:	$ 1,507	[v]

Completed Worksheet 4: After-Tax Proceeds from the Sale

Purchase price: $ 100,000   [a]

Annual appreciation rate: 5   % [o]

Holding period: 5   yrs. [n][Use Table A] (Hint: factor = 1.276)

Projected sales price: $ 127,600   [w]

Less cost of sale: __6__ %   – $ 7,656   [p]

Realized sales price: $ 119,944

Less total acquisition: – $ 103,000   [c]

Capital gain: $ 16,944

× Max. cap. gain tax (15% or 5%):   ×   15   %

Capital gain tax due: $ 2,542

Add deprec. recap. tax: + $ 4,214

Tax due from sale: $ 6,756   [x]

Depreciation Recapture	
__5 yrs.__ holding period [n]	
× $ __3,371__ depreciation [t]	
= $ __16,855__ total depreciation	
× __25%__ deprec. recap. tax rate	
$ __4,214__ deprec. recap. tax	

Note: If sellers receive cash from the sale of their investment, the tax cannot be postponed. Sellers should consider a 1031-tax-deferred exchange before selling for cash.

Projected sales price: $ 127,600   [w]

Less sales costs: – $ 7,656   [p]

Less mtg. balance: – $ 85,000   [e]

Less tax due: – $ 6,756   [x]

Net after-tax proceeds: $ 28,188   [y]

Completed Worksheet 5, Parts 1 and 2: Performance Summary with FMRR

After-tax cash flow:	$ 1,507	[v]
Investor after-tax rate of return	2	% [q] (rounded)
Holding period	5	yrs. [n] [Use Table B]
Amount accumulated:	$ 7,842	
Plus net after-tax proceeds from sale	+ $ 28,188	[y]
Total future wealth:	$ 36,030	
Initial investment:	$ 18,000	[i]
Holding period:	5	yrs. [n]
Financial Management Rate of Return (Yield)	14–15	% [Use Table A]*

* With a financial calculator, the actual FMRR is 14.29%.

■ Summary

Calculating the FMRR can be time-consuming without the use of a financial calculator. However, as demonstrated with the worksheets above, the FMRR can be calculated manually with the use of compound interest tables.

Once the FMRR has been calculated, the real estate professional can properly counsel investors about the targeted investment property. Not only can the FMRR be used to compare one real estate investment with another, it can also be used to compare another investment vehicle, such as bonds or business ventures, with real estate investments.

■ Chapter 8 Review Case Study

Using the five worksheets on pages 88–91, complete the FMRR analysis using this case study. Answer the questions on page 92, choosing the closest answer.

Property address	Smalltown Grocery Store
Buyer	Mr. and Mrs. Carlos Diaz
Date	Today
Purchase price	$2,800,000
Improvements/Land	80%/20%
1st mortgage available	$2,400,000 at 7.0%
Total equity (principal reduction)	$24,000 yearly (approximately)
Down payment (equity)	$400,000
Closing costs	$114,000
Yearly rent (potential)	$32,132 monthly or $385,584 annually.
Vacancy allowance	0%
Property taxes	$40,000
Insurance	$10,000
Utilities	$16,023
Maintenance	$10,000
Buyer's tax bracket	35%
Holding period	10 years
Annual appreciation	2%
Projected sales costs	5%
Before-tax investment rate	4.6%

Worksheet 1: Property Summary

Property address: _____

Investor: _____ Date: _____

Purchase price: _____ [a]

Add closing costs: _____ [b]

Total acquisition cost: _____ [c]

Improvement allocation: × _____ %

Improvement value: _____ [d]

1st mortgage:_____[e] × rate _____% = Interest _____ [f]

Principal: + _____ [g]

Debt service: _____ [h]

Down payment: $ _____

Add closing costs: + _____ [b]

Initial investment: $ _____ [i]

Gross monthly income: $ _____ × 12 = yrly. gross income: $_____ [j]

Annual vacancy allowance: _____ % × yrly. gross income [j] = $_____ [k]

Annual Operating Expenses

Property taxes: $_____

Insurance: + $_____

Utilities: + $_____

Maintenance: + $_____

Other: + $_____

Annual operating expenses: $_____[l]

Investor's tax bracket   _____ % [m]

Holding period: _____ yrs. [n]

Ann. appreciation: _____ % [o]

Proj. cost of sale: _____ % [p]

Inv. pre-tax rate: _____ %

100% − _____% tax bracket [m] = × _____ %

After-tax rate: _____% [q] (rounded) *(This rate is the investor's desired after-tax rate of return. This rate should be contrasted with the FMRR on Worksheet 5.)*

Worksheet 2: Before-Tax Cash Flow

Potential gross income: _____ [j]

Less vacancy allowance: − _____ [k]

Effective gross operating income: _____

Less total operating expenses: − _____ [l]

Net operating income: _____ [r]

Less debt service payments: − _____ [h]

Before-tax cash flow (BTCF):   _____ [s]

Worksheet 3: After-Tax Cash Flow

Net operating income: $ _____ [r]

Less annual interest payment: − $ _____ [f]

Less depreciation: − $ _____ [t]   ◀

Taxable income/loss: $ _____

× Tax bracket: × _____ [m]

Tax savings (if *negative*)
or tax liability (if *positive*): $ _____ [u]

Before-tax cash flow: $ _____ [s]

Add tax savings or subtract
tax liability: + $ _____ [u]

After-tax cash flow: $ _____ [v]

Depreciation Calculation

Improvement value	$ _____ [d]
Divided by economic life ÷ _____	
	27.5 or 39 years
Annual depreciation deduction $ _____ [t]	

Worksheet 4: After-Tax Proceeds from the Sale

Purchase price: $_____ [a]

Annual appreciation rate: _____ %[o]

Holding period: _____ yrs.[n] [Use Table A]

Projected sales price: $_____ [w]

Less cost of sale: _____% − $_____ [p]

Realized sales price: $_____

Less total acquisition: − $_____ [c]

Capital gain: $_____

× Max. cap. gain tax (15% or 5%): × _____ %

Capital gain tax due: $_____

Add deprec. recap. tax: + $_____

Tax due from sale: $_____ [x]

```
┌─────────────────────────────────────────┐
│        Depreciation Recapture            │
│   ____yrs.____holding period [n]         │
│  × $_____depreciation [t]           │
│  = $_____total depreciation         │
│  ×   25%   deprec. recap. tax rate       │
│    $_____deprec. recap. tax         │
└─────────────────────────────────────────┘
```

Note: If sellers receive cash from the sale of their investment, the tax cannot be postponed. Sellers should consider a 1031-tax-deferred exchange before selling for cash.

Projected sales price: $_____ [w]

Less sales costs: − $_____ [p]

Less mtg. balance: − $_____ [e]

Less tax due: − $_____ [x]

Net after-tax proceeds: $_____ [y]

Worksheet 5, Parts 1 and 2: Performance Summary with FMRR

After-tax cash flow: $_____ [v]

Investor after-tax rate of return: _____ % [q]

Holding period: _____ yrs. [n] [Use Table B]

Amount accumulated: $_____

Plus net after-tax proceeds from sale: + $_____ [y]

Total future wealth: $_____

Initial investment: $_____ [i]

Holding period: _____ yrs. [n]

Financial Management Rate of Return (Yield) _____% [Use Table A]

■ Chapter 8 Review Questions

1. What is the before-tax cash flow income?
   a. $76,023
   b. $117,561
   c. $192,000
   d. $385,596

2. What is the after-tax cash flow?
   a. $19,901
   b. $56,860
   c. $88,936
   d. $117,573

3. What are the after-tax sales proceeds?
   a. $170,659
   b. $261,361
   c. $643,824
   d. $654,000

4. What is the projected sales price? Round to the closest $100.
   a. $2,543,000
   b. $2,750,000
   c. $3,000,200
   d. $3,413,200

5. What is the total future wealth? Round to the closest $100.
   a. $1,097,000
   b. $1,130,000
   c. $1,663,400
   d. $1,800,000

6. What is the FMRR?
   a. Under 9% and 10%
   b. Between 10% and 11%
   c. Between 12% and 13%
   d. Above 14%

The Role and Responsibilities of Real Estate Licensees

learning objectives

After completing this chapter, you will be able to

■ summarize the attributes of the financial management rate of return (FMRR) model;

■ discuss the assumptions of the FMRR model;

■ evaluate the advantages and disadvantages of the FMRR compared with other yield tools; and

■ evaluate the role and responsibilities of real estate licensees in investment analysis.

■ Key Terms

interest-only loans   long-term wealth building   tax bracket stability

■ Introduction

The advantages of the financial management rate of return (FMRR) over other yield measurements have been discussed. It should be noted that the FMRR is a very flexible model that allows for many more variables than other yield tools. These variables include tax benefits or consequences of ownership, as well as negative and positive cash flows. However, the FMRR is not a perfect yield tool.

■ Assumptions of the FMRR

The FMRR uses a number of assumptions that investors and real estate professionals should contemplate before using it exclusively to measure return on investment.

Long-Term Wealth Building

The FMRR was designed for the investor who wishes to project income and expenses beyond one year. The FMRR allows the investor to contemplate ownership for an indefinite period of time. This in itself can be a drawback. As the investor starts to look into the possibilities of long-term ownership, it is difficult to project how appreciation and tax laws are going to perform. Generally, the FMRR model should be used for a five-year or ten-year holding period simply because it becomes difficult to predict much beyond ten years with any degree of accuracy.

Interest-Only Loans

To keep the discussion of the FMRR relatively simple, no calculation of mortgage reduction was considered. For the typical investment held less than ten years, the rate of return using an interest-only loan turns out be less than ½ of 1 percent different from that calculated for a conventional type loan, owing to the small principal reduction in the first years of a loan.

However, it should be noted that the impact of mortgage reduction over the long term on the FMRR can be significant. When amortization takes place, net after-sales proceeds increase, causing the FMRR to increase. Investors could adapt the FMRR worksheets provided in the previous chapter so that mortgage reduction can be considered. This can be accomplished easily with a spreadsheet.

Impact of Other Tax Deductions

The impact of other tax deductions on the FMRR was not considered. For example, many investors live in states where there is a state income tax. There may also be a capital gains tax charged by a state government. Considering other taxes on income and gain may have a significant impact on the FMRR. While increased tax rates increase the possibility of more tax savings on income, it also raises the specter of capital gains tax, reducing after-tax proceeds.

The IRS permits investors to depreciate short-term components of real property, such as air-conditioning systems and appliances. Those depreciation deductions are not included in this model. If they were used, they could increase the FMRR.

Tax Bracket Stability

The FMRR assumes that the investor's tax brackets will remain stable during the holding period. That assumption may not be correct. As an example, in 2003, tax laws changed, causing tax brackets to be reduced. But Congress can also increase tax brackets in the future. The FMRR calculation is sensitive to changes in tax brackets.

Constant Appreciation

The FMRR assumes that whatever appreciation rate is used remains constant throughout the entire holding period. As experienced investors know, real estate operates in economic cycles. Generally, real estate appreciates in value, but appreciation is subject to many local economic whims as well as other factors not in the control of the investor.

Straight-Line Method of Depreciation

Current tax laws require that investors depreciate their buildings over 27.5 years, if the investment property is residential, or over 39 years, if the building is commercial. These IRS rules are also subject to change.

Any Negative Cash Flows Are Borrowed

If the investor calculates that an investment will produce negative cash flows (that is, if operating expenses and mortgage payments exceed net operating income), the FMRR assumes that those negative cash flows will be paid by the investor using his or her own funds that would otherwise be invested at the after-tax investment rate. The cost of using these funds is the return that they would have produced if reinvested; therefore, the funds are treated as a loan. The total cost of this loan is subtracted from after-tax proceeds on the sale to ensure a fair assessment of the FMRR.

Positive Cash Flows Are Reinvested

It is assumed that all positive after-tax cash flows (the yearly net after-tax rents) generated by the property will be invested and allowed to compound at the investor's desired investment rate. Those cash flows are added to the after-tax sales proceeds to determine the total future wealth of the investor at the end of the holding period.

Current Tax Provisions Are in Effect

The FMRR is designed based on current tax laws. Tax laws change. Any revision or update should be incorporated into the FMRR calculation.

■ Responsibilities of Real Estate Professionals

Working with investors requires very different skills from those needed when working with residential homebuyers. Real estate licensees have several responsibilities when they work with consumers who wish to invest in real property.

Obtain the Skills Required to Analyze and Compare Alternative Investments

In addition to gaining field experience prior to working with investors, real estate practitioners should avail themselves of as many courses on investment fundamentals and analysis as they can. For example, on the completion of this program, real estate licensees may wish to enroll in a course on tax-deferred exchanges. This course will help practitioners understand how to help their clients postpone capital gains tax on the sale of investment property. In addition to taking courses on real estate investment principles and practices, real estate agents should learn as much as they can about alternative investments, such as stocks, bonds, and collectibles. (Resources for information regarding alternative investments are provided at the end of this chapter.) Most sophisticated investors have diversified portfolios. A real estate agent who has expertise in comparing and contrasting real estate with other investments is an agent who will develop a long-term relationship with clients.

Establish Long-Term Relationships with Clients

Agents who offer solid investment expertise are invaluable to their clients. Real estate licensees can represent consumers who are selling their investment properties and then immediately help them invest the proceeds in a new investment property as well as offer additional services to clients to enhance the relationship. These services may include appraisal, investment counseling, and property management.

Analyze Investment Potential of Various Real Estate Investment Choices

Real estate licensees have the responsibility of helping consumers understand the characteristics of various real estate investment choices. Not all consumers are suited to owning and managing shopping centers, and not all consumers can manage tenants as troublesome as the one in the movie *Pacific Heights.* Real estate professionals must understand their buyers' financial and personal profiles and property attributes to match investors to investment properties.

Communicate Investment Advantages and Disadvantages of Various Investments

Real estate professionals should be able to discuss the merits of various real estate investment choices as well as their various negative characteristics. This discussion can be enhanced by the real estate licensee's ability to provide useful information for investment decisions, including pro formas, and to use a variety of yield measurements and explain them to clients.

Seek Professional Development

Most real estate practitioners are required to participate in continuing education courses. There are numerous courses available to real estate licensees that would enhance their understanding of investments. For example, a course on 1031 tax-deferred exchanges would be a logical follow-up to a course on investment fundamentals such as this one. Courses on financing investments would also be appropriate choices for practitioners interested in enhancing their understanding of real estate investments.

Some real estate agents voluntarily participate in professional development courses that may lead to special designations in real estate, such as the highly respected Certified Commercial Investment Manager (CCIM). It is also possible to find courses that deal with specialized properties, such as farms or assisted living facilities, or with land development. (Resources are provided at the end of this chapter for information regarding organizations that offer specialty courses.)

Many professionals seek education more informally by reading specialized journals, trade publications, and newspapers dedicated to the subject of investment. They may also find experienced mentors who will provide guidance in developing investment counseling techniques. Because the investment property market is a dynamic one, real estate licensees must face the challenge of keeping their skills and education current.

Suggest Technical, Legal, Tax, and Accounting Advice when Appropriate

In most U.S. states, real estate agents have limited powers regarding advising their clients. While they may be permitted to draft contracts (or fill in the blanks) and interpret those contract clauses with which they are familiar, by and large, real estate agents are not authorized to give legal advice. Their limited exposure to tax law and accounting principles also makes them ill-suited to advising clients on the tax and/or legal consequences of owning particular investments. It is advisable for real estate professionals to encourage buyers to consult with tax and legal professionals before entering into a contract on investment property or, at the very least, to have buyers make their offers subject to a review of the terms by their tax and legal advisers. Similarly, real estate professionals should insist that sellers have their tax preparers and legal advisers review any sales agreement prior to signing.

■ Summary

Real estate professionals often feel a profound sense of accomplishment and satisfaction when helping consumers with their investment goals. Of course, it is always gratifying to earn a commission! But helping investors articulate their goals and then finding the investment that will fulfill those goals is also personally rewarding.

While understanding the various calculations and underlying principles of the FMRR model of investment analysis can be challenging, real estate agents who practice using it will undoubtedly enrich their own professional lives as well as those of their clients.

■ Web Links

For information on personal finance, go to Smart Money at *www.smartmoney.com* and CNN at *http://money.cnn.com*.

For mutual fund information, go to Morningstar at *www.morningstar.com*.

For historical stock information including charts, go to Yahoo at *www.yahoo.com*.

For money market fund information, go to *www.imoneynet.com*.

For information regarding bonds, go to *www.treasurydirect.gov*.

For information on mortgage rates and other rates, go to *www.freddiemac.com* and *www.bankrate.com*.

For information about advanced courses in real estate investment, consider these designation programs and contact the provider by going to:

ALC, Accredited Land Consultant. *www.rliland.com*

CCIM, Certified Commercial Investment Member®. *www.ccim.com*

CPM, Certified Property Manager®. *www.irem.org*

CRS, Certified Residential Specialist®. *www.crs.com*

CRE, Counselor of Real Estate. *www.cre.org.*

SIOR, Society of Industrial and Office REALTORS®. *www.sior.com*

AMO, Accredited Management Organization. *www.irem.org*

CLO, Certified Leasing Officer. *www.reic.ca*

CRF, Certified in Real Estate Finance. *www.reic.ca*

RPA, Real Property Administrator. *www.bomi-edu.org/*

SREA, Senior Real Estate Analyst. *www.appraisalinstitute.org*

■ Chapter 9 Review Questions

1. All of the following are assumptions of the FMRR EXCEPT
   a. short-term wealth building.
   b. tax bracket stability.
   c. constant appreciation.
   d. positive cash flows are reinvested.

2. Tax laws
   a. currently permit investors to depreciate short-term components of real property, such as air-conditioning systems and appliances.
   b. currently do not permit investors to depreciate air-considering systems and appliances.
   c. are not used in the calculation of the FMRR.
   d. can change.

3. Generally, holding periods of what length should be used in the FMRR model?
   a. One to two years
   b. Five to ten years
   c. Ten to twenty years
   d. More than twenty years

4. Which of the following statements is TRUE regarding mortgage reduction in the FMRR model?
   a. No calculation of mortgage reduction was considered.
   b. For the typical investment held less than 10 years, the rate of return using an interest-only loan turns out be less than ½ of 1 percent different from that calculated for a conventional type loan due to the small principal reduction in the first years of a loan.
   c. The impact of mortgage reduction over the long term on the FMRR can be significant.
   d. All of the above

5. If an investment client asks a real estate professional about the effect of an investment on the client's taxes, the real estate licensee should
   a. provide a textbook on tax law to the client.
   b. respond directly to the question with the correct answer.
   c. advise the client to seek appropriate tax advice.
   d. refer the client to the real estate licensee's CPA.

Worksheet 1: Property Summary

Property address: _____

Investor: _____ Date: _____

Purchase price: _____ [a]

Add closing costs: _____ [b]

Total acquisition cost: _____ [c]

Improvement allocation: × _____ %

Improvement value: _____ [d]

1st mortgage: _____ [e] × rate _____ % =   Interest _____ [f]

Principal: _____ [g]

Debt service: _____ [h]

Down payment: $ _____

Add closing costs: + _____ [b]

Initial investment $ _____ [i]

Gross monthly income: $ _____ × 12 = yrly. gross income: $ _____ [j]

Annual vacancy allowance: _____ % × yrly. gross income [j] = $ _____ [k]

Annual Operating Expenses

Property taxes: $ _____

Insurance: + $ _____

Utilities: + $ _____

Maintenance: + $ _____

Other: + $ _____

Annual operating expenses: $ _____ [l]

Investor's tax bracket _____ % [m]

Holding period: _____ yrs. [n]

Ann. appreciation: _____ % [o]

Proj. cost of sale: _____ % [p]

Inv. pre-tax rate: _____ %

100% − _____ % tax bracket [m] = × _____ %

After-tax rate: _____ % [q] (rounded) *(This rate is the investor's desired after-tax rate of return. This rate should be contrasted with the FMRR on Worksheet 5.)*

Worksheet 2: Before-Tax Cash Flow

Potential gross income: _____[j]

Less vacancy allowance: – _____[k]

Effective gross operating income: _____

Less total operating expenses: – _____[l]

Net operating income: _____[r]

Less debt service payments: – _____[h]

Before-tax cash flow (BTCF): _____[s]

Worksheet 3: After-Tax Cash Flow

Net operating income: $_____[r]

Less annual interest payment: – $_____[f]

Less depreciation: – $_____[t]

Taxable income/loss: $_____

× Tax bracket: ×_____[m]

Tax savings (if *negative*)
or tax liability (if *positive*): $_____[u]

Before-tax cash flow: $_____[s]

Add tax savings or
subtract tax liability: +$_____[u]

After-tax cash flow: $_____[v]

Depreciation Calculation

Improvement
value $_____[d]

Divided by
economic life ÷_____
27.5 or 39 years

Annual depreciation
deduction $_____[t]

Worksheet 4: After-Tax Proceeds from the Sale

Purchase price: $_____ [a]

Annual appreciation rate: _____%[o]

Holding period: _____ yrs.[n] [Use Table A]

Projected sales price: $_____ [w]

Less cost of sale: _____%   – $_____ [p]

Realized sales price: $_____

Less total acquisition: – $_____ [c]

Capital gain: $_____

× Max. cap. gain tax (15% or 5%):   × _____%

Capital gain tax due: $_____

Add deprec. recap. tax: + $_____

Tax due from sale: $_____ [x]

Depreciation Recapture
_____yrs.____holding period [n]
× $_____depreciation [t]
= $_____total depreciation
× __25%__ deprec. recap. tax rate
$_____deprec. recap. tax

Note: If sellers receive cash from the sale of their investment, the tax cannot be postponed. Sellers should consider a 1031-tax-deferred exchange before selling for cash.

Projected sales price: $_____ [w]

Less sales costs: – $_____ [p]

Less mtg. balance: – $_____ [e]

Less tax due: – $_____ [x]

Net after-tax proceeds: $_____ [y]

Worksheet 5, Parts 1 and 2: Performance Summary with FMRR

After-tax cash flow: $_____ [v]

Investor after-tax rate of return: _____ % [q]

Holding period: _____ yrs. [n] [Use Table B]

Amount accumulated: $_____

Plus net after-tax proceeds from sale: + $_____ [y]

Total future wealth: $_____

Initial investment: $_____ [i]

Holding period: _____ yrs. [n]

Financial Management Rate of Return (Yield) _____% [Use Table A]

acquisition cost Funds necessary to acquire investment property, typically sales price plus closing costs.

active trade or business income Ordinary income, such as salaries and commissions.

after-tax cash flow (ATCF) Before-tax cash flow plus taxes saved or less taxed owed.

after-tax investment rate The rate used by investor's to compare with the FMRR; derived from the investor's proposed alternative yield less income taxes.

before-tax cash flow A pre-tax measurement of cash generated by the property (net operating income – debt service = before-tax cash flow).

buying on margin A method used by stock market investors to buy more stock by using ownership of existing stock.

capital gain The difference between the realized sales price and the total acquisition cost.

capitalization The process of converting future income into a single present-value amount.

cash equivalents Investments in cash, such as U.S. Treasury bills, certificates of deposit (CDs), and similar investments.

cash-on-cash return A measure of the return received on the initial investment in the property. This yield measurement assumes that the investor does not pay cash for the investment property but rather leverages the transaction; also known as the *equity dividend rate* or *ratio* (EDR).

commodity A good, such as steel or beef, bought or sold in a market.

contract rent Actual rental amounts paid by tenants on signed long-term leases used to estimate potential gross income.

Coverdell Educational Savings Account A trust or custodial account that is created exclusively for the purpose of paying the qualified higher education expenses of the designated beneficiary of the account.

credit risk The risk investors take that the issuer may not be able to meet its obligation to pay the interest and repay the investment.

debt service Payments of principal and interest; mortgage payments; can be used as a monthly or annual figure.

depreciation A statutory allowance that symbolically represents the "wasting of an asset" and often has little bearing on the actual depreciation a building may experience.

education IRA *See* Coverdell Educational Savings Account.

effective gross income (EGI) Total annual income that is actually expected to be received (or potential gross income minus any vacancy and collection losses).

environmental risk The possibility that substantial costs may be required to conform to new environmental protections against risks unknown at the time the investment was made.

equity dividend rate (EDR) *See* cash-on-cash return.

financial management rate of return A sophisticated yield measurement tool that evaluates long-term income streams and derives present value.

fixed expenses Operating expenses that must be paid whether a property is occupied or not, such as real estate taxes and insurance.

futures contract A piece of paper used to represent the physical commodity being traded.

futures trading Involves speculating on the price of a commodity going up or down in the future.

generative function Retail businesses that attract shoppers to the mall. Also referred to as *anchor stores*.

gross leases Payments that require tenants to pay a flat monthly amount; often used by residential landlords.

individual retirement account (IRA) A retirement savings plan that allows individuals to save for retirement (or for college) on a tax-deferred basis.

interest-only loans For purposes of simplifying the calculation of the FMRR, a method that does not take into account reduction of principal in the debt service payment.

interest rate risk Risk related to changes in interest rates. If the interest rates available in the market increase, the value of the investment will decrease because it will be more expensive to finance the investment. If the interest rates available in the market decrease, the value of the investment will increase because it will be less expensive to finance the investment.

investment strategy A plan to develop and meet financial goals.

legislative risk The possibility that legislative changes could require additional costs for future investments or could actually increase the value of investments that were made prior to the legislative changes.

leverage The ability to borrow or use assets to acquire investments.

liquidity The ability to convert assets into cash quickly with little loss.

long-term wealth building An investment philosophy or style that emphasizes investment outlooks of five years or longer.

management The amount of effort required to find the investment and to manage it.

marketability How quickly assets can be sold at a price set by an active market.

market rent Estimated rental amounts based on comparable rental units; used to calculate potential gross income.

maturity date The specified time when the bond issuer pays periodic interest to the bondholder and is obligated to repay the value of the bond.

negative leverage The impact of borrowing when interest rates are relatively high. Negative leverage decreases the property's rate of return.

net after-tax sales proceeds Projected sales price – (sales costs + mortgage balance + tax due).

net leases Payments that require that tenants pay property taxes, insurance, and maintenance costs in addition to a base rent.

net operating income (NOI) Total annual income after paying all operating expenses (or effective gross income minus operating expenses).

neutral leverage The impact of borrowing when interest rates are neither higher nor lower than the cash return of an investment. Neutral leverage does not affect the property's rate of return either positively or negatively.

operating business risk The risk that actual income may be lower than projected and expenses may be higher.

operating financial risk The risk that available financial resources such as loans and savings may be insufficient to fund operations.

passive activity income Income received from nonmaterial participation in an investment, such as rental income, income from limited partnerships.

percentage leases Shopping center lease clauses that allow landlords to participate in gross sales. Landlords typically charge 1 percent to 4 percent of gross sales.

Ponzi pyramid schemes Illegal investment plans where money from new investors is used to pay off earlier investors until the whole scheme collapses.

portfolio activity income Interest, dividends, royalties, gains, or losses from sale of portfolio assets.

positive leverage The impact of borrowing when interest rates are relatively low. Positive leverage increases the property's rate of return.

potential gross income (PGI) Total annual income the property will produce if fully rented.

pro forma A statement providing a projection of income and expenses for the next 12 months based on trends of the previous one or two years and data from other available resources. Also referred to as *reconstructed operating statement.*

realized sales price Projected sales price less the projected costs of sale.

reconstructed operating statement *See* pro forma.

reserve for replacements An annual reserve established for the replacement of items that wear out from time to time, such as air-conditioners and heating systems.

risk The uncertainty associated with expected investment performance.

Roth IRA A type of tax-deferred savings account for individuals who meet income restrictions.

SIMPLE plan A tax-favored retirement plan that employers with 100 or fewer employees (including self-employed individuals) can set up for the benefit of their employees.

simplified employee pension (SEP) A written arrangement or plan allowing an employer, including self-employed individuals, to make contributions toward his or her own and employees' retirement plans without becoming involved in more complex arrangements.

suscipient function Retail businesses that depend on attracting mall shoppers who are passing by.

taxable income Net operating income less interest and depreciation.

taxation An investment criterion that deals with the impact of federal, state, and local tax laws on real estate and various investment alternatives.

tax bracket stability An assumption of the FMRR model that the investor will remain in the same tax bracket throughout the investment holding period.

total acquisition costs The sum of purchase price and closing costs; used to calculate depreciable basis.

total future wealth The sum of the investment's income streams, including periodic income and after-tax sales proceeds; used to calculate the FMRR.

traditional IRA A type of tax-deferred savings account for individuals who do not meet income restrictions on the Roth IRA.

vacancy and collection losses Estimated losses for unoccupied units and expenses for collecting rent based on typical management experience.

variable expenses Expenses related to the actual operations of the property that vary based on occupancy, such as utilities and maintenance.

yield A measurement that will tell investors how well an investment is performing. Yield measures the *return on* the invested dollar plus the *return of* the invested dollar.

weight-gaining operations Industries that require material that is readily available, thus favoring locations close to market areas so as to facilitate distribution.

weight-reducing operations Industries that require raw materials, thus favoring locations close to the source of the raw materials.

Chapter 1 Review Questions

1. **b.** *Capitalization rates* or *equity dividend rates* are examples of yield measurements.
2. **c.** Illegal pyramid schemes using the "rob-Peter-to-pay-Paul" principle are referred to as *Ponzi schemes.*
3. **d.** The use of other people's money is known as *leveraging.*
4. **d.** Yield, liquidity, and leverage should all be used to evaluate an investment.
5. **c.** The ability to convert assets into cash quickly *with little loss* is known as *liquidity.*
6. **d.** Savings accounts are a liquid asset.
7. **a.** Positive leverage occurs when the interest rate on a loan is lower than the projected rate of return if the investors paid cash.
8. **c.** Investors who are willing to take more risk may see higher yields.
9. **d.** None is completely risk-free. Even savings accounts have some risk.
10. **d.** Hiring property managers will have an impact on a real estate investment's yield.

Chapter 2 Review Questions

1. **d.** Education IRAs are now called Coverdell IRAs.
2. **a.** The steel in cars and the crude oil that they use are described as commodities.
3. **c.** Equity mutual funds are *not* cash equivalents.
4. **c.** "A cash asset sold by the U.S. government at auction that is virtually risk free" is a description of Treasury bills.
5. **b.** Futures are considered highly leveraged investments.
6. **d.** The best kind of IRA for taxpayers who do not meet income eligibility standards is the traditional IRA.
7. **c.** Investors who want to put their capital in the stock market but do not know enough to choose their own stocks should consider mutual funds.
8. **b.** If investors have little or no expertise in investing in collectibles or antiques, they should hire brokers and specialists.
9. **d.** Mutual funds are generally regarded as *long-term* investments and typically have *specific* objectives.
10. **b.** The paper certificate indicating an ownership of commodities is called a *futures contract.*

Chapter 3 Review Questions

1. **b.** Real estate investments have all of the following advantages except liquidity.
2. **c.** When the supply of real estate increases, values go down.
3. **d.** Depreciation deductions benefit the taxpayer, are less generous than they have been in the past, and can change by an act of Congress.
4. **c.** "Loss of value due to internal factors" could refer to bad tenants.
5. **b.** The risk that actual income may be lower than projected and expenses may be higher is known as *operating business risk.*

6. **c.** It is difficult to standardize real estate as a product because each parcel of real estate is unique.
7. **b.** During periods of low interest rates, builders tend to add to the oversupply of buildings.
8. **a.** The typical cycle for neighborhoods is growth, plateau, decline, recovery.
9. **a.** All of the following are advantages of real estate investment except detrimental tax consequences.
10. **c.** All of the following are disadvantages of real estate investment except personal control.

Chapter 4 Review Questions

1. **d.** Investment property considerations should include all of the following except commuting time from work.
2. **d.** All of the statements are true regarding fair housing laws except landlords cannot be fined or jailed for violating fair housing laws.
3. **b.** The terms *generative* and *suscipient function* are related to shopping centers.
4. **c.** The neighborhood center typically has a supermarket or drug-discount store as its anchor, often occupying around 30 percent to 40 percent of the total space available.
5. **b.** If clients are unskilled or unprepared for dealing with tenant and property problems, they should be advised to seek professional property management.
6. **d.** State landlord-tenant laws, fair housing laws, and building codes may all govern a residential dwelling unit used for rental purposes.
7. **c.** A net lease requires that a tenant will pay for all of the following except improvements.
8. **d.** A mining operation is an example of a weight-reducing operation.
9. **d.** Clients who desire attractive properties may have to sacrifice yield.
10. **d.** When a client responds to questions about anticipated performance of an investment by stating "I want a 10 percent return," the real estate practitioner should determine what yield measurement the client is using, determine if the desired return is realistic, and counsel the client if the desired return is unrealistic.

Chapter 5 Review Questions

1. **a.** The formula for deriving the cap rate is net operating income ÷ value.
2. **d.** Real estate practitioners should create a projected income and expenses statement, known as both a *reconstructed operating statement* and *pro forma*.
3. **c.** The *cash-on-cash return* is sometimes referred to as the *equity dividend rate*.
4. **d.** A commercial property recently sold for $528,000, and it has a net operating income of $79,200 per year. What is the rate of return (capitalization rate)? $79,200 ÷ $528,000 = 15%.
5. **c.** An investor wishes to purchase a $250,000 warehouse with 20 percent down. She expects that the net operating income will be $25,000 and debt service will be $18,000. What is the anticipated cash-on-cash return rate? $25,000 NOI − $18,000 debt service = $7,000 before-tax cash flow (BTCF). $250,000 × 20% down = $50,000 equity. $7,000 BTCF ÷ $50,000 equity = 14%.
6. **a.** Real estate taxes are an example of fixed expenses.
7. **c.** If a residential property has a net operating income of $49,200 per year and an appraiser uses a capitalization rate of 12 percent, the estimated property value is $49,200 ÷ 12% = $410,000.
8. **b.** A building has an annual net operating income of $10,500 with expenses averaging $2,500. Assuming a capitalization rate of 9 percent, what is the

present cash value? $10,500 NOI ÷ 9% = $116,667. (The NOI of $10,500 already has had the $2,500 in operating expenses deducted.)

9. **a.** An apartment complex contains 30 units that each rent for $400 per month. Assuming a vacancy rate of 5 percent and annual operating expenses of $54,000, what would be the appraised value with a capitalization rate of 10 percent? 30 units × $400 × 12 months = $144,000 potential gross income (PGI). $144,000 PGI × 5% vacancy rate = $7,200. $144,000 PGI − $7,200 = $136,800 effective gross income (EGI) − $54,000 expenses = $82,800 net operating income. $82,800 NOI ÷ 10% = $828,000.

10. **a.** The advantage of the cash-on-cash measurement tool over the capitalization rate method is that the cash-on-cash return method takes into account the effect of financing.

Chapter 6 Review Questions

1. **d.** The inability to calculate the impact of leveraging, appreciation, and tax consequences is overcome with the financial management rate of return.
2. **a.** A bigger initial investment is better than a smaller one is not an assumption of the FMRR. A smaller initial investment is better.
3. **d.** To calculate taxable income, investors must know the net operating income, the interest portion of debt service, and depreciation.
4. **b.** To a tax preparer, depreciation is not the same as the actual depreciation a building may experience. Tax depreciation often has little bearing on the actual depreciation a building may experience.
5. **c.** Over the years, tax laws have changed so that real estate investors have smaller depreciation deductions.
6. **d.** An investor who generates negative taxable income of $15,000 on real estate investments may write those losses off if the investor actively manages his or her properties or hires a manager, earns $100,000 or less adjusted gross income (AGI), and owns at least 10 percent of the investment properties.
7. **d.** Tax laws today require that investors depreciate residential and commercial buildings over 27.5 and 39 years, respectively.
8. **b.** Dividend and royalty income would be considered portfolio activity income by the IRS.
9. **a.** Salaries and commissions would be considered active trade or business income by the IRS.
10. **c.** Income from limited partnerships and real estate investment trusts would be considered passive activity income by the IRS.

Chapter 7 Review Questions

1. **a.** To calculate the present value of future income, investors should use the compound interest tables.
2. **c.** An example of lump sum income from a real estate investment is the after-tax proceeds of the sale.
3. **a.** An example of an annuity income from a real estate investment is annual after-tax income.
4. **a.** Table A is used to calculate future value of $1 invested today.
5. **b.** Table B is used to calculate future value of $1 invested today plus another $1 invested annually.
6. **a.** An investor purchased a $98,000 commercial building that will be held for ten years. Assuming tax laws do not change during that period, what tax will be owed on the depreciation recapture if the building is sold for cash at

the end of the holding period? $98,000 ÷ 39 years = $2,512.82 yearly deduction × 10 years = $25,128 × 25% depreciation recapture tax = $6,282.

7. **b.** Investors wish to invest $550,000 in an office building, anticipating an 8% yield. They plan to cash out within five years. The appropriate factor for five years at 8 percent is 1.469. What is the future value of their investment if their assumptions are correct? $550,000 × 1.469 = $807,950.

8. **d.** An investor wishes to have his savings total $1,000,000 before his 65th birthday. He is now 35 years old. He can invest in a bond with a guaranteed 3 percent yield. How much will he have to pay for this bond today if the factor is 2.427? 1,000,000 ÷ 2.427 = $412,031.

9. **d.** An investor believes that her real estate investment will provide an after-tax income of $2,500 annually for ten years. If her investment provides a 5 percent yield, what is the present value of that annuity income (factor = 12.578)? $2,500 × 12.578 = $31,445.

10. **a.** Investors project that the sales price of their investment will be $1,000,000 and that sales costs will run around 7.5 percent. Their mortgage balance will be approximately $250,000 and taxes due on the sale will be $16,000. What are the estimated after-tax sales proceeds? $1,000,000 × 7.5% costs = $75,000. $1,000,000 − ($75,000 costs + $250,000 mortgage + $16,000 taxes due) = $659,000.

Chapter 8 Review Questions

See worksheets on the following pages.

1. **b.** What is the before-tax cash flow income? $117,561
2. **c.** What is after-tax cash flow? $88,936
3. **c.** What are the after-tax sales proceeds? $643,824
4. **d.** What is projected sales price? $3,413,200
5. **c.** What is the total future wealth? $1,663,400 (rounded to the closest $100)
6. **c.** What is the FMRR? Between 12% and 13%.

Worksheet 1: Property Summary

Property address: _____ Smalltown Grocery _____

Investor: _____ Mr. and Mrs. Diaz _____ Date: _____ Today _____

Purchase price: _____ 2,800,000 _____ [a]

Add closing costs: _____ 114,000 _____ [b]

Total acquisition cost: _____ 2,914,000 _____ [c]

Improvement allocation × _____ 80 _____ %

Improvement value _____ 2,331,200 _____ [d]

1st mortgage: ___ 2,400,000 ___ [e] × rate __7__ % =   Interest ___ 168,000 ___ [f]

Principal: _____ + ___ 24,000 ___ [g]

Debt service _____ ___ 192,000 ___ [h]

Down payment: $ _____ 400,000 _____

Add closing costs + _____ 114,000 _____ [b]

Initial investment: $ _____ 514,000 _____ [i]

Gross monthly income: $ ___ 32,132 ___ × 12 = yrly. gross income: $ ___ 385,584 ___ [j]

Annual vacancy allowance: _____ 0 _____ % × yrly. gross income [j] = $ ___ 0 ___ [k]

Annual Operating Expenses
Property taxes: $ 40,000

Insurance: + $ 40,000

Utilities: + $ 16,023

Maintenance: + $ 10,000

Other: + $ 0

Annual operating expenses: $ 76,023   [l]

Investor's tax bracket ___ 35 ___ % [m]

Holding period: ___ 10 ___ yrs. [n]

Ann. appreciation: ___ 2 ___ % [o]

Proj. cost of sale: ___ 5 ___ % [p]

Inv. pre-tax rate: ___ 4.6 ___ %

(100% − ___ 35 ___ % tax bracket [m] = × ___ 65 ___ %

After-tax rate: ___ 3.0 ___ % [q] (rounded) *(This rate is the investor's desired after-tax rate of return. This rate should be contrasted with the FMRR on Worksheet 5.)*

Worksheet 2: Before-Tax Cash Flow

Potential gross income:	385,584	[j]
Less vacancy allowance:	– 0	[k]
Effective gross operating income:	385,584	
Less total operating expenses:	– 76,023	[l]
Net operating income:	309,561	[r]
Less debt service payments:	– 192,000	[h]
Before-tax cash flow (BTCF):	117,561	[s]

Worksheet 3: After-Tax Cash Flow

Net operating income:	$ 309,561	[r]
Less annual interest payment:	– $ 168,000	[f]
Less depreciation:	– $ 59,774	[t]
Taxable income/loss:	$ 81,787	
× Tax bracket:	× 35%	[m]
Tax savings (if *negative*) or tax liability (if *positive*):	$ 28,625 (rounded)	[u]

Before-tax cash flow:	$ 117,561	[s]
Add tax savings or subtract tax liability:	+$ 28,625	[u]
After-tax cash flow:	$ 88,936	[v]

Depreciation Calculation

Improvement value	$ 2,331200	[d]
Divided by economic life	÷ 39	
	27.5 or 39 years	
Annual depreciation deduction	$ 59,774	[t]

Completed Worksheet 4: After-Tax Proceeds from the Sale

Purchase price: $__2,800,000__ [a]

Annual appreciation rate: __2__ %[o]

Holding period: __10__ yrs.[n][Use Table A]

Projected sales price: $__3,413,200__ [w](2,800,000 × 1.219)

Less cost of sale: __6__ %   − $__170,660__ [p]

Realized sales price: $__3,242,540__

Less total acquisition: − $__2,914,000__ [c]

Capital gain: $__328,540__

× Max. cap. gain tax (15% or 5%):   × __15__ %

Capital gain tax due: $__49,281__

Add deprec. recap. tax: + $__149,435__

Tax due from sale: $__198,716__ [x]

> Depreciation Recapture
> __10 yrs.__ holding period [n]
> × $__59,774__ depreciation [t]
> = $__597,740__ total depreciation
> × __25%__ deprec. recap. tax rate
> $__149,435__ deprec. recap. tax

Note: If sellers receive cash from the sale of their investment, the tax cannot be postponed. Sellers should consider a 1031-tax-deferred exchange before selling for cash.

Projected sales price: $__3,413,200__ [w]

Less sales costs: − $__170,660__ [p]

Less mtg. balance: − $__2,400,000__ [e]

Less tax due: − $__198,716__ [x]

Net after-tax proceeds: $__643,824__ [y]

Completed Worksheet 5: Performance Summary

After-tax cash flow:	$ _____88,936_____	[v]
Investor after-tax rate of return:	_____3_____	% [q]
Holding period:	_____10_____	yrs. [n] [Use Table B]
Amount accumulated:	$ _1,019,562_	(88,936 × 11.464)
Plus net after-tax proceeds from sale:	+ $ _643,824_	[y]
Total future wealth:	$ _1,663,386_	
Initial investment:	$ _514,000_	[i]
Holding period:	_____10_____	yrs. [n]

Financial Management Rate of Return (Yield): __12–13__ % [Use Table A]

Chapter 9 Review Questions

1. a. All are assumptions of the FMRR except short-term wealth building.
2. a. Tax laws currently permit investors to depreciate short-term components of real property, such as air-conditioning systems and appliances.
3. b. Generally, five-year to ten-year holding periods should be used in the FMRR model.
4. d. All the statements are true. No calculation of mortgage reduction was considered. For the typical investment held less than ten years, the rate of return using an interest-only loan turns out be less than ½ of 1 percent different from that calculated for a conventional type loan due to the small principal reduction in the first years of a loan. The impact of mortgage reduction over the long term on the FMRR can be significant.
5. c. If an investment client asks a real estate professional about the effect of an investment on the client's taxes, the real estate licensee should advise the client to seek appropriate tax advice.